THINGS MY MOTHER TAUGHT ME

THINGS MY MOTHER TAUGHT ME

CLAIRE HALLIDAY

echo

echo

Echo Publishing
A division of Bonnier Publishing Australia
1 Centre Road, Scoresby
Victoria 3205 Australia
www.echopublishing.com.au

First published 2016
Reprinted in 2016

Cover design by Josh Durham, Design by Committee
Cover image © Mark Owen / Trevillion Images
Page design and typesetting by Shaun Jury

Typeset in Adobe Garamond and Brandon Grotesque

Printed in Australia at Griffin Press.
Only wood grown from sustainable regrowth forests is used in the
manufacture of paper found in this book.

National Library of Australia Cataloguing-in-Publication entry
    Creator: Halliday, Claire, author.
    Title: Things My Mother Taught Me / Claire Halliday
    ISBN: 9781760069995 (paperback)
    ISBN: 9781760400026 (epub)
    ISBN: 9781760400033 (mobi)
    Subjects: Mothers—Biography.
    Mother and child.
    Life skills.
    Dewey Number: 306.8743092

Twitter/Instagram: @echo_publishing
Facebook: facebook.com/echopublishingAU

For Audrey, Sean, Edie & Abbie – look back with love

CONTENTS

INTRODUCTION

History is a personal thing. I am fascinated by the perceptions people have of their own lives and circumstances.

I'm also fascinated by motherhood and the relationships between mothers and their children.

I have four children of my own, and before that, I started life as the baby of a young mother who felt she didn't have the capacity, resources, or desire to look after me herself. That led me to the home of a woman who had lost one of her own babies in pregnancy and wanted another child so badly that she was prepared to take someone else's.

THINGS MY MOTHER TAUGHT ME...

When I catch myself nagging my children about how much sunscreen they should be wearing, or how they shouldn't climb any higher on the monkey bars, or how I don't want them to go to that party at the house of a child whose parents I've never met, or when I send them away to fend for themselves in front of the television for a couple of hours while I check emails and try to find that balance between work and home, I wonder how they will eventually judge me and the job I have done as their mum.

1

Should I have shown them my tears those times I was sad? Do I tell them all the bad things that happened to me in the hope they won't make the same mistakes? Or should I do my best to show them I am breezing through life and that the world really is a wonderful place?

I have clear memories of so many moments from childhood – some good and some not so happy. There were the times we spent in a caravan together, with Mum's ham sandwiches on white bread for lunch on a flat South Australian beach, and there was the way she used to turn up the car radio and dance to Rod Stewart on the sand. Then the screaming matches between us when my idea of teenage freedom didn't match her visions for my safety. But I know there are so many other things I've forgotten. I'm sure they are all important – all memories shape us, in their own ways.

My lessons to my own children began with all the basic cautionary tales of health and safety – red means danger, wash your hands after going to the toilet, if your hair is long you should tie it back when you're standing near the stove, don't touch any spiders (just in case) and don't ever get into the car of a stranger who tells you they have a cute puppy or kitten or a bag of lollies. But life gets more complicated for our children as they grow and the lessons we need to share are forced to evolve.

SOME THINGS, THOUGH, WILL ALWAYS BE THE SAME.

When I spoke to my interviewees about the things they learned from their mothers, I was reminded that small moments do matter.

As a mother, that's both comforting and terrifying. Those times you drove them to rowing training when all you wanted to do was sleep in might actually be appreciated. That snipey little insult you deliver when you're having a bad day may be the one thing that they tell their counsellor when they're forty.

WHAT DID YOU LEARN FROM YOUR MOTHER?

For dancer Li Cunxin, they were lessons of pure sacrifice, from a mother who managed to raise a herd of children in rural China even though there wasn't always enough food to feed herself.

Ask Benjamin Law and he'll tell you that he learned about acceptance and understanding, which helped to drive his ambitions as a writer and gave him confidence to come out as a gay man.

For author Kathy Lette, the lessons were about steady support and unconditional love, and these gave her the resilience and strength she needed to care for her autistic son.

Tracy Bartram knows it was the inheritance of her mother's absurd sense of humour – even in the craziest of circumstances – that helped her become the person she is today.

A MOTHER'S INFLUENCE AND EDUCATION CAN BE POWERFUL.

In my own life, I have watched my mother overcome all kinds of challenges and upheavals. I now have even more to learn as she enters the next stage of life, bothered by the beginnings of dementia and trying to clear the hurdle of loneliness that has come with outliving her friends.

There is a lot to be gained from watching and listening to the lives that have gone before us. People may not be perfect. But even the flaws and failings have something to teach us and the happy times might have even more.

These stories aren't all dramatic. Life isn't really like that for everyone. But there is something we do all share. We all have a mother. Things my mother taught me? There are plenty. Part of growing up is recognising what those lessons were.

LI CUNXIN

Before Li Cunxin travelled the world as a leading ballet dancer and became Artistic Director of the Queensland Ballet, he spent his childhood in poverty-stricken rural China. His mother had a vision about his success, and her sacrifice for her son – to be separated from him for years when he was chosen to attend the prestigious Beijing Dance Academy – was the force that changed his life, and the fortunes of his entire family. Li's book, *Mao's Last Dancer*, was an international bestseller.

When I was younger, when I thought of my mother – or even imagined the smell of her cooking – I remembered that when she cooked, she sang. Just little tunes she made up while she worked.

She may have had a special treat of meat or fresh oil and she would be so happy because she knew we were going to have a lovely meal that everybody was going to enjoy. Now, I really enjoy cooking for my children. All my brothers have learned

Pictured: Li Cunxin with his parents Fang Reiqing and Li Tingfang

how to make my mother's dumplings. They are legendary. I don't think I can find a dumpling house in Queensland that would be comparable to my mother's.

My mother loved the arts – she was especially crazy about music. If there was any sort of performance in our village, my mother would be the first one to make us go and find a little spot – 'Just put the stool there so nobody can take it away,' she would say. We would sometimes sleep in the square. It didn't matter if it was cold or hot, we would sleep overnight there to occupy our little spot.

Mum loved to see me dance. She just loved it. Years later, she told me the story about a strange dream she had two or three weeks before I was chosen to go to the Beijing Dance Academy. One morning she woke up and told my father: 'I think our son will be selected to go to Beijing Dance Academy.' In her dream, she was in a big crowd. Because she was quite little she couldn't see anything as she tried to make her way through, so she tapped on a man's back and said: 'Hey, hey, can you tell me what is going on?' The man told her that there were some dancing goddesses. He then bent down and put my mother on his shoulders and she saw through a crack, almost in the clouds, these beautiful goddesses. They were sort of dancing and then, very quickly, just disappeared. Mum said it was beautiful – she said it was in rainbow colours and these beautiful people were wearing these chiffon costumes.

A few weeks later, a government official came to my village and said to my family: 'Your son is one of the forty-four chosen to go to Beijing to study ballet.' It was quite incredible for a peasant girl – for a peasant mother – to have such artistic dreams.

My mother was always a dreamer. I am a dreamer too. She was the one who had the sensitivity to understand our dreams. She certainly understood my dreams when I was selected to leave home at eleven years old to study at the Academy. From my village, it was a long way away – twenty-four hours on a train – and my father expressed reservations because he felt I was too young. We didn't know a single soul in Beijing and he felt that nobody could care for me, but my mother convinced him to let me go. She knew that I was a dreamer. I had big dreams as a child – more so than any of my six brothers. She said to my father: 'This is the one chance for your son, and we can't take that chance away from him.' She knew she was right. It was a chance to get ahead, do something different – do *something* – or at least not be starving back home. I did not really understand the artistic world at all, but, even then, I knew it might give me some opportunity – even if I didn't know exactly what that was.

As a mother, you know, it would have been very hard for her to let her child go, and yet she was the one who saw the big picture. I find that incredible. I have always known it was incredible but now, as a parent, there is a deeper understanding. Even when my wife and I sent our first child away for school camp – knowing that she would be well cared for and that good food would be provided – we were unsettled and worried about her being away from us. My wife and I have seen the world; we have a global perspective and we left our own homes so early on. Even so, when the time came it was hard to send our children to America on scholarships to study. It nearly killed us – and we have phones and internet and so many ways to communicate whenever we want.

When I went to Bejiing, there was no phone my mother could call me on and my family was too poor to catch the train. Even letters were too expensive to send – the price of one stamp meant several days of my family's survival. I don't know how many tears my mother shed quietly, but in front of me – once a year when she did see me – she always had a very brave face. She didn't want to take my courage away. I also think that, even though being without her son would have been very difficult, she must have slept a little bit better knowing that I, at least, had food in my belly.

Seven years is a long time to be away. Those times I did see her? Oh, they were heaven. I missed her dreadfully, especially those first three years when I was younger. People talk about homesickness as a real sickness and I can definitely agree; you have no energy, and all your thoughts are of your family – being sick is exactly what it was like. I missed my mother dreadfully. I missed her voice. I missed her smell and the smell of her cooking. It would have been different for my family. They stayed in that familiar place and only one thing was missing – me. For me, everything around me was new so it felt like a complete loss. My mother had been my strength for so long. It was her love that I longed for. Despite the tough lifestyle we'd had in that little village – all those worries about getting sick and never recovering, or starving because we had no food – my mother's laughter always made me feel that everything would be okay.

I grew up in a village of more than three hundred families and my brothers and I were all aware that we were very poor. It was tough. My mother's sense of humour nourished us: we needed it – we needed laughter just like we needed food. We would often go to sleep hungry, but with her personality and good humour, she would be able to put our situation into a context that cheered us up. She'd say sensible things like: 'Well look, aren't we lucky to be able to have at least a little something to eat? You know, others out there could be starving to death tonight.' And that was the truth, sadly. There were many people in our village who died of starvation during that time.

It was in those moments that I could see how strong she really was and how mindful she was in focusing on us and keeping us safe and happy. I mean, sometimes you only needed to look at her expression to know she was desperate, because she knew her children were going to have a tough night and not have enough food to eat, but then, somehow, she would cheer us up and make us look at the brighter side of life. It was a wonderful gift she gave to us. She took away our fears, and she never showed us her own.

It wasn't just us who got so much comfort from her strength. When people had problems – when they had a row or some family issues – my mother was always the one people would come to. She was the one people respected and she had this ability to find the right perspective on life. It was a special thing.

It's only now, as an adult, that I can truly reflect on those times and understand the power of her strength of character, of her generosity, of what a positive person she was. There were desperate moments – times when she was just absolutely on the verge of breaking down because we were so poor – and somehow she held it together and, in turn, held the family together. If she had crumbled, my whole family would have disintegrated.

My father was always similar in terms of that strength – that steely inner strength – but he doesn't speak very much. He is a man of very few words. It's always been that way. Mum was the one who was very verbal and, you know, probably because of her incredible, big personality, it created the right balance between my father and my mother. The few times when my father did speak, everybody would just be quiet – it was very effective. My father worked relentlessly and made sure that he provided for the family, but my mother was the glue.

I think I've definitely inherited a large part of my mother's personality, rather than my father's. If I didn't have that part of her, I probably would not be able to get on the stage to perform and to express myself well.

I did ask my mother, later, what her own dreams were. She told me that really, her dream was for us. She dreamed of survival for all her children and for their wellbeing, and for them to become responsible, good adults. That was her dream. It's not unusual. A traditional Chinese ideal, particularly in her era, is simply to marry well. My mother had hopes of marrying a man who would love her and care for her and, in return, she would love him and provide a family for him. My mother bore seven sons to the Li family and my father did truly love her – theirs was absolutely a marriage made in heaven. For my mother, it was a step up to a better life because her family was much poorer than my father's. She felt lucky to be with him.

After my training at the Academy in Beijing, I went to America. I think my family all had big hopes that I would do well. All my brothers had a sense of responsibility to be able to do something better to help the family but with me training for the ballet and then leaving to go overseas, those hopes were even bigger. I was probably the only chance to help them change their fate – and that's precisely what I did.

The truth is, even when I was chosen to train to dance, I still didn't know that my dream was achievable until a marvellous teacher at the Beijing Dance Academy said that if I worked hard and became a good dancer I could then help my family in return. Ballet suddenly gave me a focus and a purpose.

Once I was able to help financially, there were many things I wanted to do for my mother – buy her nice clothes, send her money so she could eat better, buy her an apartment – plus help my brothers.

I invited my father and mother to America when I was at the Houston Ballet, after I had defected, and it was wonderful to be able to do that. Mum was totally happy for me and it was probably only then that she realised there was a bigger world outside what she was born into.

Both my parents were incredibly shocked at the beginning – even seeing a refrigerator, an escalator, an elevator, the incredible offerings at a grocery store and the huge supermarkets were revelations to them. My mother was particularly amazed to be able to find cooking ingredients in the Chinese grocery stores that she couldn't normally even find in China. Even just drinking – to drink a beer at mealtime – shocked them. They were made speechless by the amount of waste in the western world. They just found it insane to find perfectly wearable clothes in the trash dumps; to throw perfectly edible food away. They were utterly fascinated and they were absolutely thrilled to see how my life had evolved.

I was always careful and I am still quite careful, really, because I don't believe in excess. I am not sure if I learned that only from my mother – growing up without anything teaches you many things. We can afford almost anything we need now but I think you still should never forget where you have come from and the values you have been instilled with. I greatly appreciate the opportunities I get today and the privileges we enjoy. You know, even wearing nice clothes, driving a car, being able to have money to go to a restaurant, or go to the theatre, or see a movie, or go on a holiday with your family – I still think it's incredible and I don't take any of it for granted.

If I had to describe my mother to someone, I would say this:

My mother was incredibly generous and had a big heart. She was kind to everyone – not just to her family. She was very resilient – both my parents have always been – but I think that was certainly the way parents of that time had to be in Qingdao. My mother always saw the glass as half full, never half empty – that was a beautiful lesson I learned from her.

When things really got tough at the Dance Academy, and even before that, I kept telling myself, you know, there are so many beautiful things in life – there are so many positive things for which you should be grateful. That was how my mother behaved, how she dealt with situations. You learn from your parents by watching how they behave – not necessarily by what they say. At times, when there was no food, my parents would just refuse to eat. They said: 'You go ahead, we are not hungry,' but you'd know the truth. We all knew.

My mother has just passed away. She was still living in China. She was happy there because there were a lot of cultural barriers for her to live a life in the West. I am always busy during the day and, even though she would be very friendly to anyone she met when she visited us here in Australia, it really was hard for her to communicate and be understood. Plus, there are six other children back in China – and grandchildren – and for the Chinese, that family unit is very important.

I saw her about once a year. It's been quite special for my children to understand how much their grandparents sacrificed, how much they've loved us and how important they've been in shaping my character.

My father passed away earlier. 'Mellowed' is not the right word, but her love for him really transformed him and I believe she helped him realise his potential as a man. He was always a decent man but through her love, her cleverness and her communication skills, he became an incredible, wonderful man.

I only remember one fight between them, when he drank too much at a friend's wedding. At the time it was the scariest moment in my life. I thought my mother and father were headed for divorce but after that, somehow, they got even stronger. For a long while after that he did not touch a drop of alcohol, and I think he realised how much he'd upset her. She made him a much better man. I think that was a wonderful example for the children to see.

One of my earliest memories from when I was a child is when I was a few years old and I went to one of my playmate's houses to play. His uncle gave him a toy car – a tiny little toy car that he had bought from the city. He showed it to me and it was something I had never seen before. I had never seen anything that beautiful in my life, so when he went to get some water for us I took that car, then I went home and I proudly showed it to my mother because I swore that my mother or my family would not have seen anything that beautiful either.

She asked me: 'Where did you get it?' and I said: 'I found it on the street.' I couldn't say I had stolen it but she knew of where I had been and who I'd been playing with, so she could see the truth.

She grabbed my hand and led me back to the friend's house. She made me apologise to my friend and his mother and then dragged me all the way back home. She sobbed after we got back because she knew she had humiliated me, but she wanted to teach me a lesson. My parents had always said to us: 'It doesn't matter how poor we are, how desperate we are, you can't lose integrity, lose dignity as a person – so never do the wrong thing.' It was such a valuable lesson. I never forgot it.

My mother was obviously proud of my career, but the fact that I am a decent father to my children and a decent husband to my wife and a decent son to my parents, as well as being a good sibling to my six brothers – I think that was probably what my mother would be most proud of. She would be happy that I became a responsible person – not a selfish one.

NAOMI SIMSON

Naomi Simson used to dream about being an artist. It was her mother who suggested a university degree in marketing, and today the successful founder of gift experience business RedBalloon is an award-winning entrepreneur and author. One of the most important lessons her mum taught her? That equal opportunity is something worth fighting for.

My mother, absolutely, is a feminist; she believes in an equal, balanced voice. Unfortunately, 'feminism' is a word that has been hijacked by some people, and repurposed as having anti-men sentiments; my mother is definitely not a supporter of those ideas. Mum knows that without the love and support of Dad – they have been married for 55 years – her life and career would not have been the same.

Mum's all about equal opportunity and making sure that everything that is available to men is available to women. Mum both worked and shared the load at home, and this made her a great role model. She led by example, and I learned from

Pictured: Lorna Elms and Naomi Simson

the early days that there could be a lovely balance in any relationship.

My dad is equally a feminist. He was always amazing in terms of washing dishes, or putting a load of washing on – he was always supporting Mum in all of the domestic duties and it was like that for all of us. We all just chipped in and no one had specific jobs. It's the same in our house today; it's not one person's job to do the cooking or do the dishes – we are all in it together and we have to pitch in.

My parents' relationship as equal partners made me sure of what I wanted for my own family. I have taught these beliefs to my son and my daughter – they are independent souls, but share my family values. I'm grateful that both my parents taught me these lessons.

In the household I grew up in, everything was equal, everybody contributed and everyone just pitched in. There was an expectation that we would take care of our own financial future.

I cannot tell you how normal that is for me. I have young women come up to me who are getting married and who didn't have mothers who were the sort of role model my mother was, and they automatically slip into doing everything for their husbands and then wonder why they are exhausted.

Mum never said: 'Don't be an artist,' but I do remember my art teacher saying that a career as an artist might mean that I would be starving in a garret. It certainly wasn't the most inspirational thing that anybody has ever said to me. That was probably when I was about fourteen or fifteen.

Mum knew that I had a creative soul but she also knew that I needed to be financially accountable for my own future, so she said she could see me in a career in marketing and sales.

We used to watch the fabulous television program *Bewitched*, where Darrin – or was it Darryl? – was working in advertising and was always drawing pictures. I thought that was what working in an advertising agency must be like, and so Mum explained to me how, in another side of advertising called marketing, you work for the business instead of the agency. It was Mum who took me on that journey and it was very much under her encouragement that I went to university.

My mum had the idea that your education wasn't finished until you finished university. The idea that high school was the end was never entertained in my household – it was just, go to primary school, go to high school, go to university and then you have finished your education. There were three stages to education and that was how it was done.

I fell in love with university – the whole idea of it. I just did the work, no fuss. I've got a B.Comm, with majors in Economics, Commercial Law, Business Administration and Marketing. I found it very interesting, but I know that I learned more during my time working for IBM in New York than I did the whole time I was at university. University sets you up with the foundation, but real world experience is priceless.

You see, in those days, you couldn't do a major in marketing at university. It was only a sub-major as part of business management administration. I remember my very first lecture in marketing because I was like: 'Finally, I am here and I have done all this other stuff to finally get here,' but then it was completely disappointing and I just thought: 'Is this all it is?' I really wasn't sure what I wanted to do.

I think when kids are in high school they are offered such a narrow view of the world. Who do you see? You see teachers, you see police, you see nurses and you don't really know what is available to you as a career. The one thing that I have told all of the young people in my life is to just be curious and interested in what they are learning at university, because it's their ability to understand and enquire – rather than what they are actually learning – that will hold them in good stead. Being interested is important. I don't know if I was particularly interested all the time, but I am very glad I can read a balance sheet and also very glad I can read a profit and loss statement – for me, economics was a generalist, broad degree that let me eventually find my passion. I'm glad Mum directed me that way.

My earliest memories of my mum began when I was at preschool – she would go off to work wearing fabulous heels and suits. I knew from a very early age that she was achieving what I wanted to achieve when I was grown up.

I always had a general idea of what Mum did. She talked about her work and she talked about it with pride, but I never knew exactly what she was working on. I do know it gave her independence – and financial independence, more importantly – and I do remember that was important because there wasn't a lot of money in our house.

She worked with computers and she used to bring home punch cards and computer print-outs that we used to draw on and use for craft. I would bring them in for show-and-tell, and say: 'Here is what Mummy worked on.' I know a lot of the other mothers didn't work.

Mum worked nine till three throughout my primary school years, so she was still always there at the end of the day, at home making dinner. Often, after school, we would go and play with a friend anyway. That's what life was like then. I think she went full-time once we went to high school.

My parents were very young when they married. My father put himself through his post-graduate degree in engineering and so he was working hard as a part-time student as well. They were both very hard workers, my parents.

These days, they squabble like children sometimes, but after fifty-five years they are a part of each other. I mean, Mum will often say: 'Oh, your father – he never stops working. He's retired and he is working as hard as ever.' And he says: 'Oh, your mother, she…' They're hilarious, but they love each other.

My dad ran a great small business. He was an expert in the area that he worked in and was very highly regarded – but he would never have grown it to be a big business. It wasn't the way he thought. My mother enjoyed being part of a bigger organisation – she worked with Aspect Computing for years.

My parents don't have a very large group of friends particularly, whereas I seem to gather people all the time. I love entertaining and I have a lot of people around – lots of family and lots of kids. It's the opposite of how we were brought up, really. Dinner time when we were kids was pretty quiet. Dad liked to watch the news and so we didn't talk much. In my own house, in contrast, there is always conversation going on and I love that.

I had the best childhood. Mum and Dad would bundle us up in the station wagon and we would go camping. Our family holidays were usually just down at Wilsons Promontory or somewhere but we always had a great time.

I travelled overseas for three years after university and my mother did nothing but encourage me. I left to travel to New York at the age of twenty, probably three days after I finished my exams. The only place I had ever been overseas before I went to New York was New Zealand. No matter what my mother's fear was about a young girl going to live in New York, she never let me know it, and now my own daughter has left to go on exchange at the age of nineteen to Istanbul. She is at Bahçeşehir University studying Applied Mathematics. I had to suck it up and encourage her and support her, and let her know what a wonderful adventure it would be, no matter how fearful I was. I guess I learned that from my mother. My mum, of course, would have preferred me to stay at home, but she knew she had raised somebody who was going to go off and have adventures, and I, too, have raised an adventurer who is going to have a big life and do wonderful things. So, my job now is to just celebrate and applaud my daughter and pick her up occasionally when she falls, but that is what we do and that is what my mother taught me – you support others to live their dreams; you encourage people to greatness and you don't let your fear get in their way.

Now that my daughter has gone off to Istanbul I've asked: 'So, Mum, how was it when I went off to New York?' She said: 'You know, in those days we didn't have internet or Facebook or anything…' I don't know how she did it as a mother.

I mean, we had letters but I was travelling in South America. I thought that I was writing them every week but I didn't realise that mail took four months to get there. When I left South America I called them and they were just beside themselves because they hadn't heard from me in all the time I had been away. I'd been writing because it was too expensive to call... In hindsight I should have just picked up the phone. Now it is just so easy for my daughter to send me a text to let me know she is okay.

Another thing I remember is that when I was growing up, Mum was angry with me a lot. I am sure ours was not the only mother-daughter relationship to be tried and tested during adolescence! I remember her saying: 'You know, you have been given the gift of the gab and you can use that for good or evil, but right now, I think it's evil.'

I was a very spirited teenager and was always challenging authority, including my teachers, so I suspect that my parents are relieved that I have turned out okay and that I have fabulous children and a job. When I became a mother, I made both my parents swear they were never allowed to tell my teenagers all the things I got up to in my teens. They've completely respected that. Still, being a parent of teenagers is not without its challenges. What do they say about the worst two years of a girl's life? When she is 14 and when her daughter is 14. My mum is pretty articulate but, even now, it's not a natural thing for her to say 'well done'. I know she is proud of me – I know – but it's not really something she would talk about.

My mum always believed in me, there is no doubt about that – she absolutely believed in me. Of course, once you become a parent you finally appreciate what your parents went through and how it is a biological love you have no control over. Your parents might not like you all the time but they do deeply love you, which is quite confounding sometimes. I think my son knows that because when he gets up to mischief, he makes sure to say: 'I know you'll always love me, Mum,' and I think: 'You bugger!'

My daughter's in Istanbul so I can't be too strict, can I? My job as a mother is to encourage my children to greatness, so when they play dumb or play small and say 'I can't,' my job is to just keep challenging them to let them discover that they can.

Mum always had a hobby on the go – sculpture, squash, yoga. She always had some creative outlet to turn to. She could knit, too – I mean, she had all sorts of pursuits. That said, I definitely didn't learn how to cook from my mother. Cooking was just not her thing. I think her attitude was: 'I have to feed these people – they need food,' and it was a meat-and-three-veg solution, really. Nothing very adventurous.

Cooking aside, I believe my mother has a high IQ and a great amount of empathy for others. She is a generous listener and she always took the time to listen to me, too. Being truly present with someone is something she taught me and I live by that every day.

I sometimes don't recognise the similarities at all between my parents, myself, and my sister. We are very different people. My parents, by nature, are quite conservative. I highly doubt either of them would be caught eating dog food on national television like I did in an episode of *Shark Tank*. What is intrinsically important to us, what drives us and how we connect with other people – we share those same ethical and family values. It is our paths that have been quite different.

But that is to be celebrated in families. My sister is solid, she is consistent. I think Mum would say I am fun.

Mum hasn't mothered me for years, no matter how I have asked for it. From the moment I left home when I was twenty, I have been independent. My parents have been there for love and support, but I am on my own journey. You have got to make it on your own. There was never any expectation that I could put my hand out and ask for any money or anything like that – absolutely, no way. Mum's attitude was: 'We've provided the education, now off you go.'

My husband and I are lucky to have all four of our parents alive. We have wonderful dinner parties about twice a year for the six of us, and that is when we get to be the children again. They are hilarious nights when we get together. I know how to have fun with my parents but it is usually when there are no grandchildren there!

I think my mum looks at her four grandchildren and thinks that they are a little wild. From my perspective, they are just who they are. Occasionally, she brings her 1950s values out to play and the kids have no idea what she is talking about. She can disconnect with her grandchildren pretty easily. This doesn't bother me in the slightest – after all, she is who she is, and she raised me with those values. Our kids will understand that in a few years' time.

When it comes to me being in magazines or on TV, Mum is so cute. We almost never talk about it, but occasionally she'll ask something like: 'Why did they choose that red lipstick for you? It's quite bright.' Despite the fact that it's not a frequent topic of conversation for us, when I go over there she's got a whole folder full of clippings from the newspaper, and she passes them over to me in case I haven't seen them – as if I am keeping a scrapbook I might want to put them in or something.

She sent me an email overnight that said: 'Somebody has remembered that I am your mother – they need a donation for a RedBalloon voucher. I told them you get these requests all the time, but thought I would ask anyhow.' My mum, I guess, is humble and proud of my success at the same time. I am sure she gets quite a kick from her friends knowing her daughter is 'that RedBalloon lady', but Mum being Mum, she would never admit to it.

I really like our time together. She recently came to visit and we had the whole weekend – just the two of us. We saw the Archibald Prize entries and we did some cooking together. We both have improved in the kitchen over the years, and I like to show *her* a few things nowadays. When the rest of the family is involved, everything kind of gets distracted, so I prefer to have her to myself. That's when she really is herself for me – not being a grandmother and not doing whatever she thinks she should be doing. She's just Mum.

We over-analyse everything these days. Back when I was a kid we just did stuff, and now we theorise and philosophise about everything we do. The truth is, we are just all muddling our way through. When it comes to family, we love them for all that they are, and all that they are not, and that is the funny thing about families. We see what they are not so great at as clearly as we see the things that they are great at – people come as a complete package and I think that is the way Mum has always seen me. She sees all of my idiosyncrasies and failings, and often, you know, family see failings more clearly than anybody else because they are concerned that you will crash and burn. They just want to protect you. They just want to see you happy, and to know that you're doing just fine.

PAUL VASILEFF

Paul Vasileff launched his first fashion collection at the age of seventeen. Today, under his label Paolo Sebastian, this Adelaide-based designer enjoys a career that sees his whimsical creations grace the catwalks of the world, as well as the figures of a growing number of high-profile actresses and celebrities at glittering awards ceremonies around the world. For Paul, the emotional support of his mum has been pivotal. But it's more than that – she's still a regular presence in his design studio, hand-sewing the intricate details that help his gowns sparkle.

M um's not just what you see on the surface. Mainly, she's this innocent, kind-hearted person but she's so funny in her own way. My friends think she's hilarious, but I'm more like: 'I can't believe you just said that.' I think that's pretty normal. No matter how much you love her, you always have those 'Oh my God, Mum – no!' moments. I do know that I am

Pictured: Paul Vasileff and Franca Vasileff

so lucky to have her in my life. I couldn't imagine it any other way and, even with her cheesy sense of humour, there's nothing I would want to change about her. She's her own person and I really love that. She's always encouraged me to find who I am. I think the greatest thing she's taught me is to be happy.

I grew up in Adelaide with two younger brothers and my two parents. Dad's Bulgarian and Mum's Italian. She was a classic Super Mum – always running around, doing a million things like cooking, cleaning, driving us around everywhere, taking care of the house and us. She always worked – she still works part-time and she helps me with my business too. My mother does a lot.

Right now, she's in the middle of two weeks off from her own job to work with me on my new collection. She's hand-sewing for me and she's quite a perfectionist. Her workmanship is amazing and I think it's something she got from her own mother. She's very precise, very dedicated, and everything she does, she does so well. That's one thing she definitely passed down to all her children – we all apply ourselves 100 per cent in everything we do. I believe it's why I've gone on to do what I am doing, why my brother succeeded with his degree and career and why my littlest brother is also doing extremely well in his education.

Mum always made a huge effort for our family. Dad worked night shifts and I remember waiting up, with her, for him to come home. We'd wait by the window. She was always the one who dropped me off at school and fortunately, in my neighbourhood, I always had a lot of school friends whose parents would drive us if we needed them to, because Mum was always busy running around somewhere.

She's a microbiologist. She is heavily involved in science but she's absolutely passionate about anything to do with nature. Mum was working full-time originally. Then, when I came along, she went part-time. She never went back to full-time again.

There are things I inherited from my mother but the science gene was not one of them. My middle brother is a chemical engineer and my dad is a chemist – I didn't get any of that. But the other thing about Mum is that she is also very good at drawing and painting and has an incredible eye for detail. Did it come naturally from her to me or was it just because she taught me how to do it? This is that question about the things you learn and the things you somehow just know. She took sewing lessons when she was pregnant with me so maybe that had an influence.

The value of treating other people the way you would want to be treated is something I've always been brought up with – something that I know Mum would say was passed down to her from her own mother, too. The importance of family and friends was another thing she was adamant about – she's always taught us to look after the people we love.

Our family here in Adelaide is quite small. When my Nonna came to Australia some of her family stayed in Italy and others went to Melbourne. Mum grew up without cousins or aunties or uncles around her all the time and that made the connection to family something that was really important. And it's not just traditional family – she believed in the idea of friends as family and holding all of them close. Family and close friends come first in our lives – before work, before anything else.

I don't remember Mum ever really sitting me down and

telling me all these things – I think it's more watching, learning from experience, and seeing the way she acts and the way she conducts herself. I see her giving so much a lot of the time and I think: 'You know, you just need to relax and think about yourself for a minute,' but instead she just does as much as she can for people – all the time.

From a young age, I think both Mum and Dad could see that I had a passion for the arts. I always loved drawing and creating and they always did what they could to help me take it one step further. Mum would organise sewing lessons or art classes – anything that she could to help support me. If Mum heard that someone was involved in fashion, or in business, she'd ask them if they would take some time to talk to me and give me advice. She's probably not the most business-minded person because she tends to give so much, but it's been a nice balance for me – I've taken those qualities from her and I feel like I run my business with a lot of heart. Some people might not think that's always a good thing when it comes to business and making a profit but it is something my mum instilled in me and that I really value.

There was this art teacher who was really fantastic and was always booked out. Mum kept contacting her and wouldn't give up. In the end, she said: 'Please just have a look at my son's work.' She ended up arranging a meeting with the teacher and she took me on as a private student. As a child, Mum would buy me pieces of fabric to practise with, and then when I was in high school I was allowed to have a fashion show as one of my subjects.

Mum was selling tickets, organising the seating – everything. Even now, with my new show coming up, she said to me the other day: 'Have you got food organised for the models? Do you need me to make anything?' She's always thinking about others.

We are very similar people and we know when we get on each other's nerves. But even if we do have occasional moments, it's all over very quickly. Out of all three of her children, none of us have done anything particularly rebellious or that we weren't really allowed to. I think Mum would be really disappointed in me if I ever touched a cigarette. Inside, I think she would die a little. It's the guilt that makes you want to do the right thing – that Italian guilt. That's something else she's passed on. It's not so much the yelling – my mum doesn't yell. It's when she goes quiet that your heart breaks.

The thing that would make Mum the most upset with us is if we didn't recycle something properly. She's very health-conscious and she's very 'green' – she's all about helping the planet. When Mum comes here to work with me she makes sure that everything that can be recycled has been recycled and if it hasn't already been, she'll take care of it. If there is a spider in the house, she won't kill it – she'll put it in a cup and take it into the garden. So now that's what I do because I feel bad if I kill a spider.

She really should've been a botanist because she knows so much about plants. My earliest memory of Mum is in the garden. That was – and still is – a happy place for her. When I think of her now, that's where I always picture her. I think she got that from my Nonno. He loved being in the garden too. Mum has a wealth of knowledge and if there's a gardening show on TV, she'll always want to watch it. That's when there's no way you can change the channel – gardening shows and cooking shows. I keep telling her it's not too late to pursue a career in gardening or botany, but I think her fear is that there wouldn't really be a job at the end of her studies – it's more of a passion.

The thing that has always stood out most for me in my career is definitely my first show. I was sixteen and had no background, no experience, no expectations, and to achieve what we achieved – and I say 'we' because, really, it was a team effort, of my parents, my family and friends – was incredible. The career highlights since have been doing dresses for the Academy Awards and dressing celebrities. As a kid, that was always a dream of mine, so seeing my dresses walking the red carpet was a kind of 'pinch me' moment. Moving to our new studio and seeing the team grow and develop has also been great.

Mum's not boastful and I think when people say something about me to her, it does make her feel awkward. I know people say to her: 'You must be so proud of Paul,' and she says: 'I didn't do anything – he should be proud of himself.' But that's not the truth. She does a lot.

Mum's very transparent in a way – in a good way. I'll say: 'Oh Mum, what do you think of this dress – is it okay?' And when she doesn't say anything, you just know. She doesn't want to say anything bad.

Her opinion matters a lot to me because she's got good taste. I know when to trust my gut as well, but I think, most of the time, I know when to listen to her opinion. I don't need things to be sugar-coated. I would rather people be honest with me and tell me they don't like something than say: 'Oh, you're fantastic – that's really good.' Maybe some people will think this sounds harsh, but Mum's not going to go and tell me: 'Paul, you can be anything – you can be a singer if you want to,' because I can't. It's reality, you know. But some parents do that to their kids. They tell them they're good at everything they ever do. Mum's honest with me, but not in a blunt way. It always comes from a positive place.

I have to say, when I have kids, I'll be looking to her as my example, asking for her advice.

There is definitely a fine line between crushing your kids' dreams and being realistic with them. I think, when I first started, that was one of Mum's concerns. She was really fearful of me getting into this industry because she had the same perception a lot of people have – that it's really quite bitchy and competitive. As a mother, she really wanted to protect me from that and although she didn't voice those concerns often, she did say to me: 'If you don't want to do it, that's quite okay.' Then, after my first show, she said: 'If you think it's not for you, that's okay as well – don't feel like you have to keep going if you don't want to.' I think, in the back of her mind, Mum was always worried that it would end with me being disappointed. I think she taught us to be really happy, confident people in ourselves – not that she's an overly confident person, by any measure, but I think because she is so true to who she is, we see she's confident in her own way.

Fortunately for me, fashion is quite a positive industry here in Adelaide and I haven't had to experience a lot of negativity. It hasn't been an easy route and it could've easily gone the other way. I am very lucky that it worked out for me – well, so far.

If I was ever upset or if I was disappointed with anything, she would always say: 'You know, it wasn't meant to be – that's fine.' She taught us that when it needs to happen, it will happen and what will be, will be. It's proven itself true so many times that now, if something doesn't work out for me, I'm never disappointed because I know that wasn't right for me and something else will happen – and it always does.

Mum and Dad complement each other well. They're happy. When Mum is running around doing a million things, Dad is the really calm and cool one, and when Dad is too calm and cool, Mum gets things organised. They're a team.

Seeing how happy they are and how well they work together makes me realise it's something I would want for myself. I don't know what it is like to have parents who fight or have major arguments. If there was any friction between them at all, it would be minor: 'Why didn't you call me when you were leaving work?' or 'Why didn't you recycle that?'

That's another big reason I haven't left Adelaide – my parents offer such a secure base for me. For my whole life, everyone has told me that if you want to make it in fashion, you're not going to be able to stay in Adelaide. I actually went to live in Italy to study at the Istituto Europeo di Design in Milan. I didn't want to go at first, but Mum and Dad kind of forced me to put my application in. Mum said: 'Just put your name down and see how it goes.' When I finally found out that I had been accepted – that I was going to Milan – I dropped the phone and Mum went really quiet, then Dad went really quiet. I don't think anyone really expected that I would be going away for a year. Leaving my family was probably the hardest thing about it.

I am glad I did it – it helped me really grow up. After living at home and having Mum prepare every meal for me, being forced to cook for myself when I got to Italy was a shock. I could make an egg and I could toast bread and that was it. I'd never even boiled pasta.

Mum came to visit me and that was the most amazing thing because we travelled around Italy and spent time with some of her family, whom she had never met. Going to Sicily, where my Nonno's hometown was, and seeing how at-home Mum seemed there – and seeing how her cousins were so similar to her, with similar mannerisms – was lovely.

When she came I had been there for six months already and I was so homesick – her visit just lifted me up again. It made everything better. I was so devastated when she had to go back to Australia.

Every day when I went home from my course, I would pull up the computer at the end of the table and call them on Skype. They would be back in Adelaide, eating breakfast or lunch and I would be eating my dinner. That's one of the main reasons I came back and one of the reasons I can't imagine leaving Adelaide again in a hurry. It's the little things, really, that you miss.

Now I'm twenty-five and for the moment I am living with my family. Sure, I might have a successful business and my dresses might be at the Oscars but, aside from that, nothing's really changed. To be quite honest, I am never really home now anyway. Mum will put my dinner in the fridge because often I work quite late.

Being close with my mum is something that I really treasure, especially since I have limited free time. If I just want to spend time with Mum, I can go and do that. It's her stability that I value most.

SHAYNNA BLAZE

Shaynna Blaze has found television fame at an age when many experienced performers might struggle to find projects. She became co-host of *Selling Houses Australia* in 2008 and joined *The Block* as a judge in 2012. This newfound fame adds a fairytale touch to a life of hard work and perseverance as a performer and interior designer, but for Shaynna it comes with its own sadness – her mum has been living with Alzheimer's for fifteen years and is unaware of her daughter's successes.

I remember, when I was pregnant with my daughter, Mum won a prize: holiday accommodation in Surfers Paradise. Mum and Dad couldn't afford to fly up, so we drove, and she got there and got out of the car and just burst into tears. It was the first time she had ever travelled. She couldn't believe she was there – to her, it was almost like Paris. I couldn't put myself in her shoes, to see what was so monumental for her. For me, it was just like, Surfers? Really? She was probably in her late forties.

Pictured: Shaynna Blaze and Annette Ainslie

My ambition was never really to be like my mum because Mum was just there. My ambitions were things I wasn't completely sure about – but I knew I wanted something more. I wanted a 'bigger' life. I can't tell you the one thing that triggered that feeling in me but I was adamant that the life I saw my mother living was not enough for me. I wanted to see the world and have adventures. I knew I wasn't the type of person to sit in the one spot and just let life happen to me.

Mum was the opposite. She didn't aspire to travel, she didn't aspire to learn more, she didn't aspire to anything other than just being around her family and friends. She didn't have a strong motivation to do anything outside the family, really. She seemed content with that but Dad was always encouraging her to get involved with other things. I think he felt the same way I do, looking back – that her world was very small. So, Mum would sign up for some crafty classes – she'd do a mosaic class or watercolour painting lessons. She painted on plates and did decoupage and that sort of thing, but she didn't really do it because she aspired to it – it was more like something to do to pass some time.

We grew up in the eastern suburbs of Melbourne and it was a beautiful childhood. We were happy. The area had been built on an old orchard, so we had a mulberry tree. It was the only mulberry tree in the area and everyone used to come and get silkworms. We also had plums, apricots and nectarines. In summer, we'd have three or four of those plastic laundry baskets just filled with plums and we'd be having plum fights in the street, all while Mum would be inside, cooking jam. She couldn't cook a main dish to save her life, but she could make cakes, biscuits, jams – and they were delicious.

I was the second child – the middle child – and always breaking the rules. Plus, I was the only girl, so I made my presence known. I was the one sneaking out, being loud, being curious, doing things differently. Mum was driven mad by me, I'm sure.

She started working later on, when we were in high school. She didn't have any qualifications or anything like that – she became a school cleaner, but she enjoyed it and made life-long friends. Before that, when we were in primary school, she was a stay-at-home mum, which is one of those things as a little kid that you don't really appreciate. You see other mums working and you think: 'Oh, I wish my mum could work,' but then, at the same time, you get older and you realise that having her there all the time had so many advantages.

It was always unconditional love from her – no matter what I did, or if she would get upset or be embarrassed or angry – there was never any question that she wouldn't still love me at the end of it. It was always like that – you always knew, no matter what you did or how bad it was, once it calmed down, Mum would always be there for you. That's probably why I pushed the boundaries so much. But at the same time, despite her unconditional love for us, she wasn't physically affectionate – at all. It was always awkward hugs. She was a highly emotional, loving person but there was usually no physical display of affection. To me, that was quite weird. My dad was the big hugger, so you'd get this big hug from Dad but you wouldn't get it from Mum, even though you knew she loved you. That was just her. She showed love in other ways. When you have your own children, you sort of look at how you want to bring them up and how you treat them and that was just one of those things that I knew I wanted to do differently. I am always hugging my kids.

Mum seemed to breeze through her life. As long as she had *Days of Our Lives* and *The Young and the Restless*, and she could socialise and make cakes and biscuits and things, that was enough for her. Mum was one of those people who was happy with her lot in life. We were total opposites. She had this very naive outlook on life, while I was always looking for the next big thing. It wasn't that she didn't care – she just went along with everything that we all did. This allowed me to be so free-spirited and to make my own major mistakes and learn by myself, which is pretty amazing. By Mum not instilling her own outlook in me, she gave me the freedom to become who I wanted to be.

The thing is, now I want to say to her: 'Wow, thanks for giving me that rope and letting me do all these things,' but I can't. She's been in a nursing home for fifteen years. She's got Alzheimer's. The best thing about getting older is being able to sit down and have a chat with your parents and say all the things you felt. But I can never have those conversations now. I realised too late. Mum has really been gone, mentally, for years.

From high school I went and studied design. At night, I was singing in clubs. I tried a bit of dancing, a bit of acting – I loved performing. Mum and Dad would come to the dodgiest bars and see me play and would sit there and smile. Mum would go up to strangers – it used to drive me nuts – and say: 'That's my daughter up there.' She was so proud. She'd come to every gig, every exhibition – everything. I don't think she was living through me – she really just loved the celebration. I can't say I was always happy about it. I'd be like: 'Mum, do you have to come?' But as much as I'd be embarrassed, sometimes I'd think that I was pretty lucky because I knew a lot of people whose parents would never turn up.

Mum was always asking me when I was going to settle down. She wanted to be a grandmother and have grandkids and she'd talk all the time about other people whose kids were having babies. When I was with someone, they were expecting me to get engaged, get married, buy a house, have kids – but I did it all the wrong way around and Mum and Dad were both unhappy about it.

When you stand there and say: 'I'm pregnant,' and both of your parents walk out the room – I think you sort of get the idea. I was twenty-three. My dad was really stubborn and wouldn't talk to me for ages, whereas Mum burst into tears. Then, two days later, she comes back, after speaking with her sister, and says: 'This is pretty exciting.' She'd just accepted it. Mum was always worrying about what the neighbours would think, so once she got over that – and, really, who cares what the neighbours think? – it was all fine.

Mum was young when she had me and I had my kids young, too. What I'm eternally grateful for is that she allowed me to keep up my career, because she'd babysit them at the drop of a hat and she would be there any day, any night – and the kids loved her. She would take them swimming and she'd take them to the movies and she gave me total freedom to run the design business I had started. Then, when my marriage broke up and I was performing at night, she was there, no matter what time of the day. I couldn't have coped without her support. I could see how much she adored my kids and having her there meant my kids were safe and happy and I was able to not only earn a living, but chase my dreams as well. It was an amazing thing. Seeing your mother look after your kids is just beautiful because you can see the joy your kids give them.

But then everything changed again.

Dad died at sixty-four. Mum got diagnosed with Alzheimer's the year after – when she was sixty-four. They were saying that she possibly had it for quite a while and he'd been the one masking it, but they also said that he wouldn't have even known he was masking it because they were just all in their normal routine. Plus, Mum was always a bit quirky. She was very forgetful, off with the fairies and, you know, she would do silly things. So the sillier she would get, the more frustrated my dad would get with her. We had no idea that what was really happening was early-onset Alzheimer's.

At first, we thought it was grief for Dad. She would miss appointments or not turn up, or buy the same magazine more than twice. We'd go over and cook her meals and the house would be really, really bad – disorganised and dirty. One of the turning points was when Dad had been gone for six months and Mum had forgotten his birthday, so we had a really bad fight – to me, the way she was acting was all bright and breezy as though she was happy Dad was out of her life. It felt at the time like she was glad he was gone and that cut right through me. Little did I know, her Alzheimer's was getting so advanced that she had even forgotten who he was. There were a couple of other things too – once, she forgot to pick my son up from day care. I knew she never would have forgotten something like that, so it was then that I knew something was wrong.

My brother and I had her tested. We watched as they asked her these simple questions, and when she couldn't answer them our jaws dropped to the floor. I knew she got muddled with the days of the week, but we all do that when we get busy sometimes. She didn't know what season it was or who the leader of the country was, or even what year it was – these were all basic things and you would never think to ask and check.

It was devastating. My brother and I felt cruel. We'd been having arguments with her and getting frustrated with her but it wasn't her fault at all. We knew she was too young and it wasn't fair. It was one of those things where it feels like the floor falls out from underneath you and you think: 'Where do we go from here?'

From there, the deterioration seemed instant. Within twelve months we had to put her in care. She actually lost her cognitive skills before she lost her memory completely. Normally, they told us, it's the other way around.

We would go out for a coffee and she would just sit there because she wouldn't know to pick up the cup. We'd be having this amazing conversation about the kids and everything else seemed pretty normal and I'd say: 'Mum, it's going cold – have a drink,' and only then realise she just didn't know she was meant to pick it up.

It was actually really dangerous. We found out later that there had been a couple of times she'd driven to the shopping centre and forgotten where she was. She'd been wandering for three or four hours but she couldn't work out how to ring us. We had to take her licence away from her before she went into a nursing home and I think that was the worst thing that happened to her. Her independence was gone. It happened so fast. She went downhill and she was just gone. By the time she was sixty-seven – just three years after her initial diagnosis – she was in the high-care ward.

My brother and I went straight into organisation mode. I had my own business but I was still working for someone else part-time. I had to take so many days off from that job to look after things, plus, suddenly, there were my kids, whom Mum had always helped me with so much. Lots of things changed in my life. We had to sell my family home. If my brother and I didn't have each other, it would have been even worse.

For the last three years, Mum has had no idea about who anyone is. The kids used to see her for a while at first but it was hard. It took her a couple of years before she started to forget who they were and then she moved into high care. My son, especially, was devastated. Now, she's totally unresponsive. Maybe a few hums and other noises but that's it. She hardly ever opens her eyes.

And the sad thing is, my life is so crazy with travel that I might have months where I'm only home one day a week, and when I'm home I want to see my husband and my kids.

It's horrible to think of Mum as a burden, but you just have to feel comfort in knowing she's really well looked after and that you should spend the minimal time you do have with the people who are there with you – people who need your support and attention. Still, the guilt about it when you're not there – it's overwhelming.

I think the whole thing has taught me how resilient I am. That's one of the biggest lessons. As much as I always thought that my mum wasn't that important in my upbringing and I always viewed my dad as the defining person in my life, I know

now that there were so many qualities she had that I dismissed and I think that's what gets me really sad – knowing that she's alive, but not alive, and that I can't thank her. Looking back, I think Dad died with a lot of regrets because I don't think he ever achieved what he wanted to. Yes, he was more creative and, sure, he might have lived a more interesting life, but Mum was there unconditionally – and always with a smile on her face. But I can never thank her for it now. I think that's the hardest thing.

It's one of those things you can't predict. I've always tried to look after myself health-wise, but sometimes, no matter what you do, it comes down to whatever cards you're dealt. I don't mean that it's like: 'Well, I might as well drink and smoke, because I'm going to die anyway.' What I get out of it is that, rather than regretting what I do and don't do, I celebrate what I have right now and just make the most of it.

Mum may have never been ambitious but she was always just happy to be surrounded by love and balance and stability, and to me those are really important things. I've got an amazing husband now and amazing kids. It's an incredibly balanced emotional foundation that allows all of us – not just me – to go off and do things ourselves. It's how I've been able to have this shot at a TV career that has been so wonderful, and I realise now how important that is. I certainly never appreciated the value of it when I was younger. No matter how much you want to achieve and what you want to do, that core balance always has to keep you grounded.

Now, I think I'm sort of in that holding pattern of waiting for Mum to die, which is a horrible thing. It's about not knowing whether I will actually mourn her or whether I've already done the mourning – whether it might be a relief, in some ways. I just don't know.

I've had time to reflect on her a lot and what she's lost and what she's missed out on and I know I get a little bit angry. Not at her but I get angry at the universe, at just how unfair it is that she's missed out on seeing her grandchildren really grow up. But I'm sure a lot of people have that. My daughter has these little funny quirks that just remind me of my mum so much. They could've had a lot of fun together.

What I've missed out on is the opportunity to speak to my Mum and say 'I'm sorry' for certain things and 'thank you' for certain things. I want to be able to say: 'Let's go to see a movie together' or: 'Let's go see a play,' because she loved musicals – because I'd like to spend some time just being mother and daughter.

I think the defining moment for me was having my kids – that gave me something to answer to. I've always wanted them to have someone to look up to and I do my best to give them total unconditional love and total acceptance no matter what they do. That's all you can do – be the best you know how to be. Being a mother is all about learning, all the time. Being a daughter, I think, is too.

TRACY BARTRAM

Tracy Bartram's diverse performance career has extended to live cabaret, top-rating breakfast radio, singing, and a co-hosting role on cooking show *The Intolerant Cooks*. There have been raucous times and sad times, as well as a successful battle to overcome the addiction issues that ran in her family. Throughout it all, Tracy's relationship with her mum hasn't always been happy – but there's always tomorrow.

I t was a crazy household.

My father was an alcoholic – and a very unwell alcoholic, which is a tautology because all alcoholics are unwell – and I think the first thing that springs to mind is that my dad would go into these rages and punch holes in walls. We lived in a flat in Dandenong – a 1960s thing with hardboard floors, beautifully built – and Dad would just punch holes in the walls. Then my mother would very carefully take pictures out of magazines and put them on the wall with sticky tape, all over the place,

Pictured: Edward George Bartram, Tracy Bartram, Stephanie Bartram, and Kellie the boxer.

covering these holes. So you'd have a picture of Normie Rowe out of the *TV Week* on an angle on the wall and another one at the bottom of the door and no one ever asked why they were there. If we got home and there were new posters up, we knew Dad had been on a bender. It may not sound like it, but this is a happy memory.

We used to go to church on Sundays and even saying that sounds strange because we weren't a religious family. My mother had been raised in a Catholic convent but she didn't practice Catholicism at all. I was baptised as Church of England but we went to the Methodist church around the corner because it was a two-minute walk.

My mum and my girlfriend's mum would walk up and down the street a hundred times – talking all the way – but they would never come in for a cup of tea. I'm sure it was because things were really bumpy at home. Whenever my dad would go into one of these rages, my mother would just spontaneously start singing: 'With Jesus in your heart, it's a happy, happy home,' and we would just scream laughing. Her way of dealing with a crisis was to laugh about it and I think that was the biggest influence she's had upon me. We have always shared this ridiculous sense of humour and we are both very loud laughers. We are just raucous. We're not melodious like magpies – we're more like cackling crows.

My parents are cockney so I grew up with cockney humour and very British humour – *The Benny Hill Show* and *Morecambe and Wise* were regular viewing. What I remember most is us rolling around laughing at stupid things.

We would have the radio on all the time at home, and the first song I remember hearing was 'She Loves You' by the

Beatles. I was three. I remember that coming through the radio and thinking: 'Wow, that is just so great,' and then, years later, I remember Mum came home with the single of 'Help Yourself' by Tom Jones. Mum and Dad cleared the furniture and pushed the green lounge suite with the bendy timber arms to one side and they danced around the lounge room.

When they were courting, they danced. Even when we were in England, when I was very little, I can remember they would go dancing. Mum would have on her beautiful lemon chiffon gown and I'd say: 'Mummy, Mummy, twirl around for me.' I thought she did it like a princess. I remember little black court shoes with diamantes on the front and Mum always looking so amazing. She was gorgeous. Dad wasn't drunk all the time. He would have long periods of abstinence – or it would seem long at least – but when things were good, they were mad about each other. Totally co-dependent but happy.

Someone said to me recently: 'Oh my God, you are exactly like your mother,' and I said: 'Well, you wouldn't say that if my father was here.' It's interesting that I'm told that I look like her. I have her legs and her cheekbones – I'm sure she would like them back. She is the runt of the family – she is only five foot nine and I am six foot one.

We are both really passionate about animal rights, to the point where we think other people are really strange who don't put their animals first. You know, I would quite often be late home and I'd say: 'A dog got run over and I had to stay with it till it died,' and she wouldn't bat an eyelid. My father was ropeable that we had become the lunatic fringe – going to animal rights protests together – but we didn't care. It was like we had found this thing that we could do together and we were really heavily involved. We used to go to meetings at the RSPCA and Mum was quite the activist. She taught me about values and about standing up for what you believe is right.

I saw her hit him once. You know, Dad shoved Mum and she shoved him back and I remember thinking: 'My God.' He was a very big man – six foot five – and she just shoved him back in the chest and said: 'Don't you dare.' What a brave woman.

I am sure some would say she wasn't brave at all to put up with it but I saw her step into her power and she was like: 'How dare you – how dare you treat me like that,' and that was an eye-opener.

My father hit me – he used to hit me a lot – but he has been the only one. I hit him back because I got sick of it, but it is a horrible thing to hit people. I've always been staunchly anti-violence.

I remember being at some seminar once and someone saying: 'The only reason we hit children is because they are small enough – you wouldn't go up and do something to an actual colleague just because they pissed you off but we do it to little kids because we can.'

Another thing Mum taught me was, no matter what, you just keep on keeping on. I remember on their twenty-fifth wedding anniversary, they had a fight and Dad didn't end up going. It was at The Village Green in Mount Waverley and it was quite ritzy. I was working there as a barmaid and I'd booked a table out the back in the nice bit. Before they had the fight, I'd worded up the band and halfway through the dinner, they called out Mr and Mrs Bartram to dance. Mum had to dance with my friend Robbie – who was, like, nineteen – because Dad didn't show up, but she kept smiling and she had her frock and she was going to go out and have a lovely time. And she did. I remember that was pretty gutsy because we did have a good time without him. I think at that point she was used to Dad not showing up to things. She probably just thought: 'Bugger it – I am still going to go.' She could be very tough.

My mother became an orphan at fourteen. She was an only child and her father had suicided, a fact she didn't find out until she was seventeen. She was at someone else's funeral and a family member said something like: 'Well at least he didn't top himself like your dad.' That was the first she knew about it because her parents had separated when she was little and she hadn't seen him again.

When she was eleven, she contracted polio. She went to hospital and after a year they told her she could go home. She said: 'Will I have to wear those callipers on my legs?' and they said that yes, she would. And then she said: 'Then I am not going home until I can walk out of here.' I don't know a twelve-year-old now who would say that. She stayed in hospital for another two years – three years in total – and when she was fourteen she walked out of there with no callipers. If you saw my mother's legs even now you would have no idea that she'd had polio. She's got great pins. So there she was – she'd fought this amazing battle and she was finally back home and her mother died six months later from a cerebral haemorrhage.

Her mother had come from quite a big family, and so my mum was given the choice of living with either her mum's favourite brother, who was a lorry driver, or rich uncle-so-and-so.

Mum chose her mum's favourite brother, and so she went there to live with him and his two children. In those days you had to crank the lorries to start them, and one day he was cranking the lorry on the side of the motorway and someone fell asleep at the wheel and he was killed. My mum went through enormous trauma.

Unfortunately, her uncle's wife was quite the tyrant and was brutal towards my mum. Real Cinderella stuff – scrubbing the floors and all. She married Dad pretty much as soon as she met him. She was desperate to get away.

When we came out from England we lived in a migrant hostel. I was three. I don't remember all the stories of my mum's life being laid out in front of me but I know I would have asked my mother about that sort of stuff because I was one of the only kids I knew who didn't have grandparents – they were all dead.

I was always asking Mum things about her life – I liked trying to piece the stories together. Once I met Mum for lunch and said: 'How come you talked about doing the catechism and the stations of the cross but I wasn't raised Catholic?' And she said it was because after the war, the Catholic school education was the best education and I said: 'Okay,' but she went a little bit pink and I knew I was onto something.

So I asked her if her mother was Catholic and she said no, and she went a little bit more pink. I said: 'Was anyone Catholic? If you're not Catholic, and my grandmother wasn't, was my great-grandmother Catholic?' Mum said: 'No – she was Jewish.' I went on: 'That means I'm Jewish and you're

Jewish,' and she said: 'Hmmmmm, we don't talk about that.' We have never talked about it since.

I rang all my Jewish friends and said: 'Guess what, I'm Jewish!' and they were like: 'Gevalt! You live in East St Kilda and you eat cheese blintzes for breakfast and you're doing stand-up comedy – we knew you must have been one of us.'

I decided that I wanted to go to the shul, and so my friend took me to what was meant to be a liberal shul. I got there and all the women were on one side and all the men were on the other. The rabbi came up to us and when I went to shake his hand he recoiled, as if I had a serpent in my hand, and said: 'You don't touch the hand of a Rabbi.' When I asked why not he said: 'You could be menstruating,' and I went: 'You won't shake my hand because I could be menstruating? Well, fuck you, Rabbi!' Everyone went 'Ooohhhhh' and I just walked out. That was my entry into Judaism.

When I married my second husband, we smashed the glass and I wanted to own that – but I did put it in a plastic bag because I didn't want to leave glass under the rotunda. It actually felt really good to do that sort of ritual thing, but that's about where I left it – although the bloodline makes my son Jewish, there was no way I was going to circumcise him.

I identify myself as a metaphysician. I just happened to be born Jewish. I am a Pom who grew up in Dandenong and I teach metaphysics, so really it doesn't mean anything to me.

Mum is a very vivacious woman – even at nearly eighty years old. She is still really beautiful, too. At one point, she wanted to join the local bowls club but they wouldn't let her wear dangling earrings so she didn't join. She always was quite the conscientious objector. She bowls at a place where she doesn't have to dress in whites and observe all the strict rules. I think white should be banned, anyway. It makes everyone's arse look big.

I'm not sure what her ambitions were before becoming a mother. She was twenty-three when she had me. When she was in her mid-fifties, and I had started my career in comedy, she decided she wanted to try acting.

I was having breakfast with a bunch of performers this one time – some really great people – and I said: 'Oh, I am going to go and see my mum in this play today, she is doing this female version of *The Odd Couple*.'

I was worried that she would be terrible, but my actor friend said: 'Don't worry, she will be.' I said: 'Well, what am I going to do?' and he said: 'It's really simple – when you see her, you just say, "Hey Mum, what about you!" You might have to say it a couple of times but that is all you have to say.'

So, off I went to see my mum on stage. It was probably the worst thing I have ever seen – it was torturous. It was directed by a friend I have known since I was five, and my mother was there smoking because she was playing the Oscar character and I was watching my mother smoking on stage and it was just – awful. Then, afterwards, I was standing in the foyer and Mum came out and I said: 'Mum, what about you!' and she said: 'Thank you, darling.' Again I said: 'What about you!' and that is all I said. She was so happy.

I grew up watching Lucille Ball and my mother was very physically similar to Lucy – you know, very tall, very slim, used to wear the pencil skirt and flats and all that stuff. Mum has got the klutz gene – seriously, if she could bump into it, or fall over it, she would. One time she was cleaning the toilet with Harpic and it wouldn't come out of the bottle, and when it finally did come out it went into her eyes and I had to take her to hospital. Dad was there anyway – he'd had some minor operation for, I don't know, a charisma bypass or something – so I thought, well, while we're there, we'll see him too.

I rang for an ambulance – 'My Mum's squirted Harpic in her eyes' – but in the end I rang a taxi and all the way there I was thinking that she was going blind. Then, when we got to the hospital, I wheeled her around to see Dad and he burst his stitches because he was so angry that my mother had ended up in hospital with Harpic in her eyes. That pretty much sums it up right there.

Another time, she was up in the roof rescuing baby birds and her foot came through the ceiling. Bang. It was just hanging there, like a scene out of *Arrested Development*, you know. It's like the blind leading the blind. This ridiculous house with a clumsy mother staggering around breaking things, and a raving lunatic Basil Fawlty-type character that happened to be my dad.

Mum and I have always had periods where we lose contact with each other – I move away or one of us has upset the other. I'm in therapy because I deal with the fact that I have come from a family that's been affected by alcoholism. Alcoholism is a family disease and it affects everybody and I remember one therapist saying to me years ago that when you grow up, there is no glue to keep you together as an adult. That aspect of my childhood was very painful for me and I left home when I was seventeen. Looking back, I am not sure what Mum thought about that but I wanted to go. We are both mothers now and my son left home at twenty – I thought he wasn't ready, but it was a different world then. I think we were much braver and we didn't have the internet and all that stuff to scare the shit out of us. We were fearless and we had great music and the only real drugs around were alcohol and pot – it was a different time.

If I really have to examine it, I think that because my mother didn't have her mother from the age of fourteen, she wasn't given the guidance or the tools to learn how to deal with the uncomfortable things and so, like many of her generation, the easiest thing to do was to not deal with it. I've spent a career laughing about it on radio or in shows but it has broken my heart more than I care to talk about, really.

We go years without talking to each other – she just cuts me out and won't talk and I won't know why. A couple of days after my last birthday I decided to just turn up on her doorstep. So I went with some flowers and some chocolates and some hand cream. I went knock, knock, knock on her door and she said: 'Oh, hello darling,' as if I had never been gone. We watched a movie on the telly together, had a few laughs, a bit of a chat, then I left. Who knows what happens next? That's what it's like.

I have a picture of me when I was five, holding my little baby sister – she's probably nine months old and all chubby like a doll – and I'm just beside myself. You can see it on my face. I remember looking at that photo and thinking: 'I'm going to have my own baby one day and I'm going to be a really good mum.'

I wanted to be a mother from the time I was five, but when I was nineteen I was told by a doctor: 'Look you'll never have children and you should have a hysterectomy.' At that point

I'd already had three years of treatment for problems with my fallopian tubes, but I just said: 'I don't believe that.' I remember thinking: 'Okay, I will have my baby when I'm thirty-five,' and I just stored that away and got on with other things. From the ages of nineteen to thirty-four I saw naturopaths and read books and learned lots of things about natural health and how to look after my body. And I had my baby, Max, when I was thirty-five.

I feel like I'm a natural mother. I love being Max's mum and I miss him terribly in the sense that I am not there with him in the way I was when he was little – he is twenty-one now and independent, off at uni and doing his own thing.

I had my own problems with alcohol but I believe in that philosophy – 'Give me a child at seven and I will show you the man.' I remember thinking, I have got to stop drinking before Max gets to seven because I will have broken him. He's turned out brilliantly – although, being my son, he'll probably end up in therapy, too. He's six foot four and such a spunk – an amazing man. Being his mum has been the best thing I've ever done.

I would love to be one of those women who have an amazing relationship with their mother but I don't have that. My mum knows that I love her – I think that probably she just finds me really confronting. I remind her of my dad. It's been challenging but I know in my gut, the same way I knew with my father, that everything will be reconciled on her deathbed. Whatever needs to be done will be done. It's my karma, you know?

NAPOLEON PERDIS

His career in the makeup industry started from
humble beginnings in suburban Sydney, as the son
of hard-working immigrants. Today, with more than
eighty-five of his Napoleon Perdis concept stores
dotted around the globe, this boy from Paramatta
says it all began when he made-up his mum's face
before a night out at the local Greek dance.

When he was happy with her, Dad used to call her 'my
Elizabeth Taylor'. Mum would always wear lipstick,
mascara, blush – everything. She was stunning. I used to be
completely mesmerised when I watched her getting ready – the
way she turned into this glamorous creature. It was so fun to
watch. But when Dad was in a hurry and he just wanted her
to be ready? He'd say: 'Operation Christmas tree – come on!'

Mum was born on an island called Kythira, which was both
Italian- and English-occupied and wasn't given to Greece until
the early part of last century. Mum and Dad didn't believe in
arranged marriages, which was something a lot of other people

Pictured: Napoleon Perdis and Liana Perdis

in their family did. In fact, their relationship was considered evil by my mum's family and my grandmother. They didn't want my dad at all. He wasn't from the same island. Back in Greece, Dad had actually been part of the socialist, enlightened movement and during the civil war, when he was nineteen, Queen Frederica saved his life and exiled him to an island called Leros. He was educated and given his degree then left to come to Australia because things were tough in Greece in those days.

The only reason my parents met is because, in Dad's shop that he'd opened in Paramatta in Sydney, he had the very first TV in the area. He used to invite Mum over to watch it and afterwards, he walked her home. After three or four walks, he asked if he could kiss her, and her mother saw them. His experiences made him very different from the other men my mum had met and they both fell in love. Three months later, they had to get married – their parents were so embarrassed about their relationship that they put the pressure on.

Mum's family had come to Australia before Dad, and she had been exposed to more Western culture than he had. She demanded that he get her a ring when she got married. She was also very into make-up. Her auntie had been her mentor and had taught her how to put on lipstick and use face cream, and it was something Mum always cared about a lot. It made her feel special. She liked looking good.

One of the only reasons Dad would get angry at her was because of her make-up. To open up the shop at 6 a.m., they had to leave home at about 5.15 a.m. Mum would get up so early, just because she wanted extra time to do her hair and all her make-up. She would spend ages.

It was a very modest three-bedroom, one bathroom home.

My two grandmothers were in one room, my mother and father were in another and my brother and I were in the other one. In the morning, you could hear the rustling of her getting ready to leave with Dad.

I remember her coming in to our room – coming over the bed just to give us a little kiss on our foreheads – and you felt that comfort. Everything was more glamorous and beautiful when Mum was around. It was something that I really longed for and I wanted to see her at the end of the day.

She would go in and set up that sandwich bar and serve the customers and whenever we went there after school, it was so wonderful to see her and she would always smell wonderful – not of the traditional sort of cheap hamburger smell that most of those shops had.

Mum was always very nurturing. She would be working in the cafe with us by her side and she would be so busy serving customers and cooking, but she would still always listen to our stories about what we did at school that day. She had this way of making us feel like we had her whole attention.

There are times that I remember feeling a bit lonely. Mum and Dad had to open the shop early and we wouldn't see her until the afternoon. Our grandmothers were there to make sure everything was running well but, you know, when you're a little kid, sometimes it's just your mum's face you want to see most. And the times when she was there – oh my God, it was like Christmas. She would want to spoil us and look after us and cook for us and do all these special things because she knew that we missed her – and she missed us.

My parents ran that shop seven days and seven nights, probably up until I was sixteen years old. On the weekends it was different, because Mum would go in and help Dad open up but she would finish at twelve o'clock, just before lunchtime, and she would come home to us, just as we were finishing Greek school. Then she would take us to do Greek dancing and we'd have the whole Saturday afternoon with her. Dad was never really around until a lot later – and by that time I was almost married – so that time spent with Mum was always really precious.

She was one of those ladies who took a real pride in her home. Every season, she'd change pillows, or she'd change the couch around, or change the decorations that went with the table. On weekends, she would cook Greek pastries and on special occasions, like Easter and Christmas, there was always something home-baked.

Being involved with the Greek community was really important to both my parents and at the end of the day on Saturday, we would take a change of clothes down to my dad at the shop and he would change and we'd all go out. Saturdays were always really glam days to be with Mum – she would dress up and do her hair and make-up and put jewellery on. She looked so beautiful. We would be with our cousins, our friends – lots of people from the Greek community – dancing, eating and just celebrating life.

And then Sunday? That was work. We'd all go in to the shop together and my brother and I would both help out serving so Mum and Dad might have a little rest.

They used to have these special cocktail party functions in the Greek community for people who had just arrived from Greece. One night, Mum had a beautiful new dress that she had made and she was going to do her make-up. I was reading this magazine with tips on how to do mascara and eyelashes, so I said to Mum: 'Can I do your make-up?' And she said 'Okay.'

It definitely wasn't my best work. She looked a little bit like a drag queen. The brow was overdrawn and she had a bit too much shadow but to this day, I'll never forget that she never discouraged me. She wore it out just the way I did it.

I remember, specifically, that a couple of women actually said something to her about it. Some of them would turn up their noses at Mum because she always wore make-up and was a bit freer with her Western ways – Mum was always the one who would tell dirty jokes – and also because she had married Dad and it wasn't an arranged marriage. They said to her that night: 'Your make-up looks very strong,' but she still didn't say anything about me doing it and she didn't wipe it off. I think it was her way of being very proud that I did her make-up and it really gave me such a sense of confidence. I remember every detail of that function: the blue dress she wore, the patent leather shoes, her stockings – everything. One of her accessories was a little necklace that Dad had bought for her and the whole thing made such a special impact on me.

I thought: 'You can do your hair, you can do your dress, you can have your shoes and your jewellery, but the whole story only comes together when you do the make-up.' I could see her being complete.

To Dad's credit he didn't say one thing about it. He probably thought to himself that her make-up was too heavy but he kept quiet. He didn't say: 'Oh don't do that, boys don't do that,' or any of that stuff. It was really the turning point that set the pace for me – a turning point that would set the pace for my whole career.

When I decided to do make-up professionally, Mum was supportive. I had finished university and had met my wife and I told my mum my plans and all she said was: 'That's a good idea.' The next questions were about how I was going to set it all up. Being Greek, she wanted to know how I was going to turn it into a business – making sure it would also become an income-earner for me.

You know, wives have a very strategic role in creating a balance with their husbands, as long as it is a reasonable, loving marriage. When I wanted to start my own business, my mother basically said to my father: 'I don't think this is one of those fleeting moments for Napoleon – I think this is a moment that is important to him.'

Mum always had a strong influence over Dad. I think he was quite infatuated by her glamour. She was thirteen years younger than him, as well. She just said to him that she thought it was one of those things that I really needed to explore and that I was passionate about it. Mum was there to give me the emotional support, and my wife, Soula-Marie, was there to give me all the structural and logistical support that was so critical. I had two special people who believed in me and that was really important.

Mum was a catalyst for Dad being pacified and allowing it to happen. It was amazing and I'm always so grateful for that. If she believed in what I was doing, she would always help and she would just make sure Dad understood. It was like her magic spell. She communicated with Dad in a way that bridged the gap between being in Australia and the old ways from Greece.

I started door-knocking, from florists to beauty parlours with bridal salons, and I would ask if I could do a complimentary make-over for them, next time they had a bride coming in for a trial. By the time I had knocked on five doors, someone said yes. That's how my business started.

Most Italian or Greek or Lebanese immigrants from that generation – they always helped their children set up a business, if they could. My parents had saved to do that too but the whole idea of me starting a make-up business was a lot for my dad to get his head around and invest in. Mum said: 'Let's just give him a chance,' and so, instead of giving me the $60,000 they had planned to give me, they cut that sum in half and gave me $30,000. Mum negotiated that with Dad. I was a bit scared of the risk but I used that moment to launch internationally and that was the beginning of Napoleon Perdis as it is today.

I think Mum always wanted to be an accessory or fashion designer but in Greece, when she was a young girl, her father committed suicide. He had emphysema and he thought he was going to be a burden on the family. My mum and her own mother found him and that was something that tormented her. She was just a young girl, seven years old, and basically, she did what the family wanted her to do – immigrate to Australia when she was seventeen and just survive. I think she lost a lot of her dreams.

As Mum became more upwardly mobile as an immigrant, she was passionate about being more glamorous and that was how she expressed herself. She was happy to be a housewife or a business partner to Dad but she'd said goodbye to any other real ambitions. The only goals she really had were for her kids to go to school and do well and go to university. She didn't get those same chances to be educated and she really loved the fact that Dad was so smart. It wasn't that he was smarter than her – she was smart in a different way – he'd just had different opportunities to gain formal, intellectual knowledge.

It wasn't always perfect between us – me and my mum. Like any teenager, I did things that my mother didn't like. I started smoking quite early and that was a rebellious moment for me. She was not happy. She didn't like a couple of the girls I had dated earlier on, either, because she thought they were taking me away from my studies. Generally, though, Mum and I had a very similar philosophy about what sort of things we liked in life and what sort of things we didn't, so we always got along much better than I did with my father. My relationship with him took a long time to become mature and to reach a level of real understanding – I think because he was always very confronted by me.

I am probably stricter than my parents were with me. I've moved my family from Australia to Los Angeles, and then to Greece. My girls having spent so much of their childhood in LA, we've done whatever we could to protect our family values. My wife and I had to work to protect our Australian cultural values. My wife was always the one to bring in sandwiches or Anzac biscuits on Australia Day or Anzac Day to the school in Beverly Hills where they were. Really, they resented our push to make them so Australian because, to them, they were California girls.

Because I didn't want to lose those values I cared about, I was ruthlessly strict in many ways. My wife was brought up in Athens until she was fourteen, when she came to Australia, so for us, with our own children, it was a case of honouring our own Australian-ness, and our culture as Greek Australians. I guess I remind myself more of my father in that respect, because he was the one who was very strict about making sure we respected our Greek cultural heritage when we were being raised in Sydney. Dad was strict about lots of things and I suppose, because he worked so much, it was a way for him to have an influence on our lives, even when time restrictions meant he wasn't always able to be physically with us. My mum used to give me a lot more freedom.

As a father of four daughters, a really important thing for me was to make sure that my girls understand their value as women. No one can actually tell them what to do or control them. My wife is a strong woman and I think my mother has been a good role model for them in that regard, too.

I can't speak for everyone's relationship and I don't want to generalise, but I do think daughters-in-law connect more with mothers-in-law once they become mothers themselves. At first, Soula-Marie had to really set the boundaries – she didn't want my mother coming over to cook for us and clean for us and do all that. Her attitude was that she and I would share the tasks of our home, which I found quite challenging because I had a mother who was always spoiling me at home and doing everything for me.

My mother ended up really respecting her. Then, when we had our first child, they bonded in a new, deeper way. My wife really believed in the Greek tradition of naming the first daughter after the husband's mother and because she stuck to those traditional beliefs, my mother saw her as a woman of real values. Today, my mother would call my wife for advice – even though we live overseas and Mum is still back in Sydney – much more than she would call me.

Mum has a very important role in my daughters' lives. When the girls were developing breasts, they were kind of hunching over and all embarrassed and my mother would be the one who would help them feel proud. She'd say: 'It's natural, don't be ashamed – you've got to wear a bra you can feel comfortable with.'

Mum has all these little philosophies about how she thinks the girls should be. When she was here in Greece for five months, they kind of loved that she still cares about her appearance and doesn't let herself go. They love that she's accessorising, wearing beautiful necklaces, and how her bag matches her shoes. They always say to her: 'You look so beautiful,' and she basks in that because, as a mother to two boys, I think she is really loving the chance to be more feminine and talk about things that she couldn't discuss with us.

My girls like her because she is not coming from a traditional Greek grandma perspective – Mum has a modern outlook. She would never say to them: 'Don't wear those shorts.' Instead, she says things like: 'You have beautiful legs, you show them.'

Because Dad never restricted her being beautiful and sexy around him, she feels that her granddaughters should absolutely embrace their looks, know their value and make it part of their strength – not something that takes away from other aspects of them, and not something to feel embarrassed by either. That's been interesting for me to watch because it's something only a woman of experience can pass on to young women.

When she's angry with me, Mum might complain that she

sees me all the time in photos but she doesn't ever see me in person. She tells me that she wants to hear my voice. She's torn between accepting me as an adult male who's making his own decisions and moving around the world in his own way, and still seeing me as her little boy who will always be there for her. We have that little struggle every now and then – I love her and she loves me but she can cut me down. Once, when she was being a bit nasty and angry, she said: 'It doesn't matter who you are – at the end of the day, we're just village goat-herders and I don't want you to forget that.' And I'm, like: 'Sure Mum, but I don't need to be out buying goats to appreciate those village values.'

I know it's hard for her, having us all so far away from her, but for us, really, Australia is still always home. My girls already have a foundation of being Australians through me and my wife, and it is important for us that they have a connection with being Greek too. They will always be Australian, just like I am, but with a global outlook.

Australia is a great country. I mean, it's a place where my grandmother first came and could only sign her name with a circle. My family went from that to putting us through tertiary education and giving us support and encouragement to follow our dreams and be successful and happy.

I love that Mum can now spend all the time she wants with us here in Greece and that she doesn't have to work anymore. If I had one wish, it would probably be that Mum didn't have to work seven days and seven nights for twenty-five to thirty years. She's got terrible varicose veins because of standing for so many hours behind a counter, and she's had three operations on them. In those days, the immigrants did everything themselves – they mopped, they cleaned, they set up shop and they did it day in, day out. If Mum just had a few years where she was able to rest her legs and not have to be standing from so early in the morning to so late in the evening, she probably would've had much better health.

I chose to be very ambitious and a couple of my daughters may also be very ambitious – and a couple of them may not be – but if there was one main thing I learned from watching my mother, it's to try to create that balance and not allow my ambition to take over everything when it comes to children and my personal family life. Life is so short. You can't get those years back again.

FIONA PATTEN

The beginning of Fiona Patten's life in politics was as the CEO of the Eros Association – the peak body representing the Australian sex industry. Fiona's political career took off when she became founder and leader of the Australian Sex Party, and she is currently a member of Parliament in Victoria. Her mother raised her to be well-mannered, well-educated and well-travelled. But when it came down to sharing the more intimate details of her life in public, her mum was less enthusiastic.

M um brought out the wooden spoon without any problem. She didn't just threaten with it, she used it. She felt that there was nothing wrong with punishment. When I got caught smoking, she made me sit in my bedroom with the windows closed and smoke a packet of cigarettes. That worked for a couple of weeks.

But she was a very friendly and happy person and she would wake us in the morning in good spirits. I don't think she was

---

Pictured: Ann Patten and Fiona Patten

overly affectionate – I don't ever remember my family being touchy-feely – but she was one of those 'just get on and do it' type of people. Mum was very sort of English in that way – you know, stiff upper lip and let's just go.

She also was the one who got up at five o'clock in the morning and took me to swimming training and drove me to swim meets three hours away on a Saturday. She was a very dedicated mother in that way and she saw it, really, as her job to do that.

My mum was English. My dad was in the navy and he was stationed in Scotland. They met, fell in love and married and then, for their honeymoon, they took a ship to Australia. My mother had never been here before and she didn't know anyone and, really, she didn't even know Dad that well – she'd never even met my dad's family.

Mum was twenty-one when she met Dad. Her upbringing was as part of an upper middle-class Scottish/English family and she'd been to finishing schools in Europe, so I don't think Mum had any real ambitions, except to get married.

They moved to Canberra, of all places. This was in the early 1960s. My mum had spent a lot of time living in London and so this was quite a change for her. I was born shortly after that. My sister was born eighteen months later, and my brother a few years after that.

When we were really young my mother didn't work, although she did take on part-time jobs from time to time, but because Dad was with the navy we travelled a lot. We travelled between Canberra and Sydney, we went back and forth between England and Scotland, and we lived in America for many years. My mother was really attuned to this lifestyle because her father had been in the army so she had travelled all her life. We grew up in Canberra, Sydney, London, Washington.

Mum was very matter-of-fact, so there was just no question that there was going to be a problem. I don't recall ever going to a new school thinking: 'I wonder if I will make friends.' I think it was like: 'I will go to a new school and make friends.' She never, ever gave us any doubts. Mum loved travelling and I still love travelling today.

Mum travelled so much that she was used to always getting to the next destination and she had strategies in place for meeting people. She had a lot of close friends through my dad's work, as well. There was a group of naval wives who travelled and had children around the same age – she had a group of very dear friends. Quite often they would find themselves all in England together, even though they were Australian, or they might all be living in Washington at the same time.

Probably the hardest move we ever made was coming back from America. We had lived there for four years and that was the longest any of us had ever lived anywhere in our life. And I was aged between eleven and fifteen – the incredibly crucial junior-high years. I had just got into high school, plus I looked like I would qualify for the nationals in swimming, so there was a whole bunch of stuff I felt attached to. I think it was also the hardest move for Mum. It was a very wrenching time for all of us.

When we were in America, every weekend we had a chance to we would take the pop-up camper to a national park or to a historic town somewhere and she would never miss an opportunity to do these things. Mum would have loved to stay living in America – she was very sad to go. When we got back to Australia, she went straight into full-time work and started a career for herself, working for a telecommunications company. I think it was her way of keeping busy.

She was very keen for us to have extracurricular activities. Every single place we went, particularly for me, there was sport and Brownies and Girl Guides and those sorts of things. I think it was good for her, too, as it enabled her to meet people and get to know the neighbourhood. I probably take after her a bit in that way. I like being busy.

We used to have swimming or soccer training after school every day and swimming training before school, so I don't think we particularly noticed her working later and not being at home waiting for us. Maybe my brother noticed more because he was younger. I mean, at that age – as a teenager – I didn't want to be anywhere near my parents. She was always quite rigid about everyone doing their fair share and she probably became more rigid about that when she started working. Her time to handle all the domestic stuff was obviously more stretched than ever.

I think I do have a tendency to just say yes to lots of things, which can put me in really good situations, and occasionally in not so good situations, but I do think the travelling gave us all a little bit of faith in ourselves and enabled us to be quite independent. Because we were regularly the new kids, we all developed a strong resilience.

'The Talk' happened after she found a whole bunch of condoms in a wastepaper basket in my room. Mum and Dad had been away for a weekend or something and I had stayed home and obviously had a friend over. Mum sat me down and told me that they'd been using condoms before I was born, but when they thought she was pregnant they stopped using them. As it turned out, she wasn't, but they thought: 'Oh well, bugger it, we're not using condoms again now.' And that was how my life started. There was no way they were going to have a child at that stage, otherwise. I was born in their first year of marriage and that wasn't the plan but once they'd thought she was pregnant they got all excited and changed the plan. So when Mum found condoms in my room she knew what that meant – she didn't want me to get pregnant young. She must have had some regrets about her own life not turning out the way she had originally intended.

Mum had had other boyfriends but she'd never had sex with them. Dad always said that she hadn't had sex with him before they got married, despite considerable effort on his behalf. Oddly enough, that conversation was in a letter he wrote to his parents when he announced that he was getting married. When I was ten I found I letter he wrote to his parents saying that there hadn't been much to write about but that now there was a bit of news: 'I have met this wonderful woman – her name is Ann, she's gorgeous, she's a virgin (despite my best efforts), with child-bearing hips, and I will love her till the day I die.' It was hilarious but lovely.

When I did get pregnant later and I had to have an abortion, that's when I found out that Dad had got another woman pregnant – weirdly, she was called Fiona – and they had to go through a backyard abortion. Finding out things like this about your parents is strange in some ways, but it does give you the bigger picture of who they are, and why they parent you the way they do.

Mum and I had a fairly tempestuous relationship from when I was about fifteen until about twenty. Around nineteen it got very bad, so my father stepped in and I started having a weekly lunch with him. He would report back to Mum about how I was and what I was up to.

Looking back, I think I was just doing my own thing. I was going to university, I was going out and I had broken up with a boy whom she really liked. I suspect that she would have hoped that I married the bank manager's son – she liked him very much – but then I started going out with a guy she liked a lot less and that's when we felt like we were really drifting apart.

It's a bizarre story – this new guy's father was a doctor and when she had first come to Australia, he was her first doctor. When she was pregnant and she didn't really know anyone, apparently she felt that he abandoned her because during her pregnancy he went on to become an anaesthetist. She felt that she'd been dropped by him and, secretly, she'd never actually forgiven him – and then she transferred all those feelings onto his son.

Originally, I wanted to be a landscape architect. Mum was very pleased until I changed to industrial design because that is what my boyfriend at the time was doing.

I think she was just generally worried about me – she probably thought that I wasn't on a great path and that I was partying too much and maybe, you know, just being a bit of a bitch. I thought she was trying to boss me around too much.

I was very raucous and probably did get up to a bit of mischief in those years. In fact, I *did* get up to a bit of mischief in those years. Mum caught me selling marijuana at one stage while I was still at home. I was in my last year of high school and my boyfriend – the one that she liked, actually – and I had got some hash to sell so we could have a holiday when we finished school.

That wasn't good. She had no experience with drugs of any sort. She absolutely freaked out and thought that this was the end – that the daughter she knew was bound for hell. She really didn't know what to do and at one stage she was thinking of ringing the police to make me own up, but she thought better of that and actually rang a drug and alcohol counsellor, which was great. They spent most of the time counselling my mum – telling her that it wasn't heroin.

I had about five hundred dollars cash in my top drawer and Mum took the money as punishment, but gave it back to us later so we could have our holiday at the end of the year.

Mum's life experiences were so different from mine. Up until my late teens, our life experiences had been quite similar – we'd moved, we'd gone to new schools, we'd travelled and all of that – and then, I guess, when we began to have less in common she worried that I was going on a different path and probably not a very safe path. Later in life we kissed and made-up, but even back then, really, she was always there if I needed her. I would even get weekly food packages.

When Dad retired, they bought 100 acres and ran it as a B&B homestead. They had separate units and she loved that. She loved craft and when she was at home she was always doing something – a pottery course, an upholstery course, a sewing course. She made our clothes and she taught me to sew as well.

When I was at uni and I left industrial design, I switched to fashion design and ended up with my own fashion business. I don't sew as much now but I did sew a dress last year – it is a skill that I obviously still have.

Mum loved having dinner parties and she was a good cook. I am the same but probably a bit less in recent years since I've been in the world of politics. I think work takes over your ability to cook a three-course dinner for people.

When Robbie Swan and I launched The Eros Association, the *Sydney Morning Herald* ran a front-page story about it that started with: 'Former sex worker, Fiona Patten,' and one of my mum's friends faxed it to my mum.

That was a difficult phone call.

She said: 'I have seen you in the paper today.' I think I was just sort of hoping that, because she lived on the south coast, she wouldn't see the *Sydney Morning Herald* and everything would be fine, but no – she did see it. She said: 'How could you?' She repeated it over and over.

I went down to see them soon after that – not because of the article, just because I was going down there – and that is when Mum started grilling me.

'What was it like?'

I think because it was 'former', it was actually also easier for her to cope with. I told her: 'It was just something I did – I didn't do it very much and I don't do it any more.'

I have no doubt that it was the last decision she would've wanted me to make. But it wasn't really a decision I deliberately made – I kind of fell into sex work. I was doing outreach at the time and it was like: 'Oh, there's no one here to do the client – all right, I'll do it.'

I guess that sort of 'get on with it' approach to life and to everything was one of the reasons I did just say yes on that day.

I think, at that stage, Mum was quite happy with her own life and she knew I was happy. She was absolutely in love with Robbie, my partner, and I don't think she particularly judged me on it. I was twenty-eight. I know that she was somewhat embarrassed by it, but she knew that Robbie and I were having a good time.

Her asking me about what had happened was more out of curiosity – 'What about if you're with an old man or something?' During this conversation my father was asleep in the chair and his false teeth had slightly fallen and we looked at over at him and my mum went: 'Aahh,' and just sort of nodded and it was hilarious. Then she didn't really want to talk about it. My dad definitely didn't want to talk about. I think that he dealt with a few things that way.

When my sister, Kirsty, came out as gay, my mum couldn't deal with it but my dad could. It wasn't that they were worried about her being gay – they were worried about her happiness. She probably had a few bad choices of girlfriends at that time and so my parents didn't warm to her choice of partners, but then once she started going out with Linda, the woman who remains her partner today, everything changed.

I remember one Christmas and Linda was coming with Kirsty. Mum always insisted on Kirsty having single beds set up in her room. I got the double bed with my boyfriend – there was even one time I didn't bring a boyfriend and I still got the double bed and my sister got the two single beds. When I found out Linda was coming I made a point of telling Mum: 'Look, if you don't give them the double bed then I'll give them my double bed.' But to her wonderful credit she had already done it, which was really lovely and made Kirsty feel fantastic.

Because she went to boarding school when she was only seven, my mother never had a close relationship with her mother. Her father was in Germany doing repatriation work after the war and there were no schools in the area they were in, so they found this French convent and Mum was sent there. My grandmother used to go and visit her a lot.

My grandmother was not that maternal, but she was born in India and when she turned seven she was sent to boarding school in England, while her family stayed in India, and then moved to Hong Kong. She saw her family maybe once a year. I think it's what you learn.

Mum got very sick seven years ago, about a year and a half before she died. It was all prior to us setting up The Sex Party and I still hadn't moved down to Melbourne then.

Unfortunately, my dad also died before we got into the elections. He was around when we set up The Sex Party and he helped us with that and was very good, but he wasn't quite like Mum. He sort of took more of a backseat on things like that.

I really, really still miss her and I think a lot about how she would be involved in my life right now and how much fun she would be having with it. She would've loved helping out; she would've managed campaigns for me, without a doubt. She would have done anything she could, whether it be letter-boxing or handing out leaflets. It was one of the saddest things that she wasn't around because I think she would have really enjoyed the fact that I was in Parliament.

Mum was a wonderful organiser and she had a very practical way of looking at things – if you had a problem, she would always have a straightforward solution. 'Let's get going' – that was Mum. I think she instilled that in me to the point where I don't like sitting around. I can't really lounge around at home in daylight hours. I hear her voice – 'What are you doing there just sitting around? Get up and do something.' As a newly elected Member of Parliament, it is quite a good voice to hear.

When I used to ask my brother and sister about this, they always said that Mum was embarrassing because she would put a lot of demands on people. For example, when I got engaged to this fellow she didn't like, she immediately put ads in the paper celebrating the engagement; she immediately bought me an engagement gift and started getting my whole family to send me engagement gifts because she knew that the minute she started doing that, I would started getting cold feet – and she was absolutely right. She told me, one day, that had been her exact strategy. She knew it would cause me considerable consternation and, indeed, I moved out and I never married the fellow. I went overseas with my grandmother instead. Mum, sometimes, was very cunning. But she did it for the right reasons.

TIRIEL MORA

Tiriel Mora grew up surrounded by iconic figures of the Australian art scene, thanks to the connections of his parents, Mirka and Georges Mora. His acting career was nurtured in backyard play productions and home movies and, as an adult, he has featured in some of Australia's best-loved films and TV shows, including *The Castle* and *Frontline*. Life with his artist mother has been one surrounded by books, paintings and plenty of conversations. And in between? There have been a few food fights.

I cannot tell you how many times it has been said to me: 'It must've been absolutely fantastic to have Mirka Mora as your mother.' I say: 'Yes, but it was also challenging – sometimes, more challenging.'

It's possible that Mirka related to people in a different way, so they saw a very different side of Mirka than I did. As a kid, you had to see the side of her that was your mother – a mother with a reputation for being different.

Pictured: Tiriel Mora and Mirka Mora

A lot of people use the word 'eccentric' but I don't buy into that. I think there's a lot more to it and I don't think that's on the money at all.

Mirka was – and still is – just an extraordinary individual. There's no one else like her and that should be celebrated. It just took me a while to understand that.

My mother was at a birthday party for one of my friends once and she picked up some food and threw it at someone else. Then it was on. Food fight. Cake flying everywhere. I went through stages in my childhood, and certainly in my teenage years, of being embarrassed by some of those antics but, at the same time, I could see why she why she would be doing that. I could see past it because, let's face it, food fights are fun. I've started the odd one myself, on set. That's Mirka's influence.

Georges couldn't help but have a certain etiquette and correctness about him – ethics and morality and all that more conservative stuff. He was a huge contrast to Mirka in that way. I got a little bit of both of them.

Being outrageously creative – and just outrageous – was normal behaviour from my mother when I was growing up. Lots of fascinating, very bohemian stuff happened down at the beach house, which seemed normal to me. We'd see Charles Blackman painting a nude, but he was actually painting a nude – he was painting on a naked woman in the living room.

There's a lovely photo in Mirka's memoir, taken at the house on the beach at Aspendale in what would've been the early or mid-sixties. It's of Mirka and Mary Perceval and I'm there with Alice Perceval, who was my childhood sweetheart. Mirka has dropped her clothes and she's showing her bum to the camera as a kind of joke, but if you look at the two kids, we're just completely oblivious. That was my childhood.

Mirka liked to shake things up a bit and shatter that staid, conservative kind of mindset. She liked to rebel against that, expose it and challenge it.

I've got Mirka's sense of absurdity and I like to think that I am capable of spontaneity. Mirka's extroverted in many ways, and likes to be the centre of attention, so I've got a little bit of that but that's also tempered by shyness. I'm not self-conscious – I mean, you can't be an actor and be too self-conscious. That freedom to express myself is very strongly influenced by Mirka. She also instilled in me the importance of belief in oneself. I think if you give a child belief in themselves that's a really, really significant thing. There's a fluidity about what constitutes ego and what constitutes belief in oneself. It's a fine line. It needs to be a healthy belief in oneself, as opposed to a delusional kind of thing. Being an artist, and choosing to express that the way you want, does require great belief in yourself. It's a very similar thing with acting too. You get rejected so many times but you have to be resilient. That's another thing I think I got from Mirka – her resilience. If you look back on what she went through in her childhood and what she was able to achieve – it's amazing.

After escaping the Nazis in France – escaping the death camps – she bounced back. When they got to Australia after the war, it must have been like an opportunity to remake yourself, in some ways, or to really be yourself. I think there was an incredible freedom in that. But that was in the context of a very conservative Melbourne in the early 1950s, so she had to rebel against that too. When it came to the way she mothered us, she wasn't following any set rules on what she was meant to be like. An artist will often sacrifice certain aspects of their other life to concentrate and focus and be devoted to what they're doing. If she analyses her own approach, she'll say that her art comes first and the kids come second, but she'll also say: 'Oh, I was always painting with you in my arm.'

As for the stories of her childhood, she didn't talk about them a lot. I think much of it was very painful for her. That's often the case when people have something traumatic in their family history and it makes it difficult to share. It's not much fun to go over those experiences and try to relate them in a way that doesn't terrify your child. It's not so much about family mythology, it's more about the fact that these are the experiences we come from and this explains why we are the way we are and why we take this positive and constructive approach to being in this society. Georges was very reluctant to talk about his experience in the French Resistance and maybe he didn't want to make it sound more adventurous than the hell war actually is.

I've used the word 'resilient' about Mirka before and she is – there's a stoicism, a survivor element there, that was in both of them. That's a pretty important thing to hand down to a child. You can't force a child to have empathy but you can expose them to ideas and thoughts and other people's situations, where empathy is the primary response and the default position – those were things that were handed down through the experiences of both Georges and Mirka from their lives during the war. I've never understood the term 'tolerance' when you talk about people coming from different cultures to Australia. I think the word should be more like 'acceptance'.

My feelings of Mirka were always really affectionate and she spoiled me rotten. There was always classical music playing and she would explain the stories behind the pieces – embellishing with more details about what the composers were doing and why there was a focus on this particular instrument or that one. I couldn't help but have an enormous respect and love of art. I never felt that I was worse off because Mirka was an artist – there were many more positives to that than negatives. I can't think of any negatives at the moment but when I was younger I know there were times I did.

I wouldn't let Mirka walk to school with me because of the clothes she wore – space boots and crazy stuff like that in the sixties. I had a conservative desire not to stand out. I didn't want to be ridiculed because my mum dressed funny, or just because those kids up the street wouldn't understand a bohemian artist. The idea of being yourself would've been a big shock for those kids.

But even though there were those times when I didn't want to draw attention to myself, thanks to Mirka I did have the capacity to be myself in primary school. It was a wonderfully positive thing – a reinforcement in that belief in yourself and that concept that no idea is unworthy of contemplation.

Mirka would always come out with some left-field view on a problem. So, as a teenager, if I asked her about girls or relationships, she'd come out with something absolutely unusable. What was great about it was that she came up with stuff you just wouldn't expect. But then I'd go to Georges and get a more sensible opinion.

I had a kind of independent existence, growing up. Mirka lived up the road when I was about eleven and we lived with

Georges in a hotel in St Kilda. The waitresses were like our big sisters – Georges was overseas a lot. I would go to visit Mum just to hang out in her environment because her environment was fantastic – but part of the joy in being part of it was that I could then leave it and come somewhere that was calmer and less chaotic.

Before she lived up the street, it was very clear that their marriage was over. There was more conflict than harmony so, for me, it was actually a relief when she left – the tension had gone. Mirka was definitely happier there too.

Georges was my Rock of Gibraltar. He represented everything solid in my life. Mirka was not that. Not at all.

This probably sounds very sad but it took me until I was around eighteen to appreciate my mother as a person and as a mother. I think, before that, I found her to be much like a piano – beautiful but challenging. I was fascinated but I didn't really understand everything about her.

She didn't always provide everything I needed growing up. There were lots of amazing things that were provided, of course – and now I am so grateful for all those layers that were added to my life. But back then, I really just wanted a mother.

I used to enjoy going to friends' places and having the white-bread experience – that very normal view into normal childhood. Because most of our other friends whom I knew from my mother and father's circles – they weren't normal at all.

That's the irony – that the white-bread view of Australian life was becoming exotic for me. I could see the good sides and the bad sides but even then, even though it was calmer and quieter and more organised, I came back thinking: 'You know, this is actually pretty good, what I've got.' My childhood was culturally privileged in pretty much every way. I was exposed to great artists, great art, incredible music and books – that makes me very, very lucky. And lucky to have survived, too.

It was always about looking for a balance. Schoolwork was always very important for Georges, but for Mirka, making jokes, having fun and being open-minded was just as important. When it came to what I wanted to do in life and the approach to education and creativity, my parents had very different views. Georges would always say: 'Read, read, read,' and Mirka would always say: 'Draw, draw, draw.' I was somewhere in the middle. Mirka was always saying: 'You're not writing enough – are you drawing?' Meanwhile Georges was wanting me to go to university and have a back-up plan, and I think he was right. I am sure Mirka had an opinion but she always trusted Georges' judgement too. In terms of the discipline you have to embrace at uni, and the way it broadens your horizons, it was a wise thing.

Mirka always loved painting. For me, I love acting – being in films, doing TV, plays, anything as long as it's acting. And I don't mind not being paid much, because I couldn't bear doing something else. Mirka always pushed the creative stuff. When I was little she always bought us special pens and paper and wanted us to draw, or I would write poetry and she would always make a fuss about it and want me to do more. She still asks me: 'Are you writing? Are you writing?' But it's a very hard discipline.

When I turned nineteen I spent a year in London, but for me, the crucial part of that move was that I no longer had the same expectations of this person as a mother. So that freed me of a lot of stuff that can get in the way of understanding Mirka as a person and as an artist, who happened to be my mother. For me, my relationship with Mirka got better once I was an adult and didn't need the same things from her that I'd needed when I was growing up.

Today, it's great. We go to lunch together, we talk, we laugh and it's wonderful. You know, the longer life goes on, the more respect I'll have for Mirka. I see all her attributes now.

She likes to play the naughty grandmother and she does that very well. My daughter, Audrey, is nine, so she's pretty sharp and she has very, very clear perspectives on things. She adores visiting Mirka because it's a wonderland. Her place is full of amazing stuff and a lot of books and masses of paintings. We were talking about it the other day and Audrey said: 'I think Mirka's house is 80 per cent paintings, 20 per cent other stuff.' I think it's 50 per cent books, 40 per cent paintings and 10 per cent antiques and other odd things – but whatever way it adds up, it's a fascinating environment for a kid. Now I see it through Audrey's eyes, I think that's what Mirka wanted for me when I was growing up – just a fascinating, stimulating environment. I've never been bored visiting Mirka.

It's so hard to compare the childhood I had, and my experiences, with those of my own child – I mean, it's not possible. Life is very different now. It's not fair to say to my daughter: 'Oh, we had so much freedom, we could do anything we wanted to – and we did.' I feel so protective of my daughter, and the way we used to be just down on the beach all day, doing our own thing? Life's not like that any more.

I have told her a few stories – the food fights, her grand-mother pushing this grand dame of Melbourne society into the pool at a party – just little droplets of bohemia. There are so many stories of mum that my daughter will learn – from me telling her or what she sees in books. Of course, not all of those stories are true.

In the last thirty years, there have been so many books come out on the history of modern Australian art and the role my parents and their friends had in it all. I've been in the very fortunate position of being able to read what other people think – plus I had my own narrative running inside. I am in an unusual position because I can't help but see my family – my mother – historically because that's the way other writers and academics and observers have seen it. So I am kind of influenced by what they have written, put together with my own memories. I have a multidimensional view of my life and my relationship with Mirka.

I remember sitting at the dinner table and there would be the art critic Robert Hughes and all sorts of people there. It was a privilege to listen to them talk about art and stuff like that but then Georges always expected me to make a contribution as well and not sound stupid. I probably wouldn't have it any other way but there was an element of there being great expectations of us from a fairly young age.

We were exposed to stuff that children aren't normally exposed to. The dramas of artists, alcoholism, hiding whisky bottles from certain artists if you knew they were about to visit. These were dramatics and theatricals of adult behaviour that we thought were normal in so many ways, because kids are resilient like that – oh yeah, okay, no biggie. But the opposite would've been very mundane. Just an ordinary childhood where nothing really happened. I wouldn't change a second of it, really. I became an actor because of that upbringing.

Down at the beach house, we'd do little plays – all the Blackman kids, the Perceval kids and us. In our social circles, it seemed quite a natural thing to perform. We knew that it could be therapeutic, in many ways. It's an awfully tough business and, of course, my father was right – I should've got a law degree.

One of the most important things Mirka says is that you never stop learning. Recently, she told me she is still discovering the power of how colours work with each other. She says that you keep discovering. That attitude has always kept her evolving and it certainly corresponds with acting. I don't think you could ever reach the point of saying: 'Oh, now I know it all.'

There was a shift between really appreciating her as a mother and really appreciating her as a person – and then, of course, really appreciating her as an artist. That took me a while because, if you are the child of an artist, it's very difficult to be completely objective and look at the art as if it were the output of someone who is not your mother. I suppose in my early twenties I started to really appreciate what she was doing and that's been a fantastic journey for me as the years go by.

Obviously, I've got works of hers from many different periods – ranging from when I was a little kid to more contemporary stuff – and her work, her style and her visions have grown on me. As time goes on, I think: 'My God, she's actually a fantastic painter,' and I was slow to come to that realisation because I had trouble being objective about what she does. The more grown up I became, the more I understood what she was doing – what she was looking for.

With my own career, she's embarrassingly proud and she's always gotten a great kick out of seeing me on telly. I think she kept a scrapbook for a while and I think she actually likes it.

It's always been easy for the press to love Mirka. She's provocative and charming. Over the years, she sort of cast a big shadow over the family – and Georges had a big shadow as well. So, maybe she's glad that the kids did okay for themselves. I suppose all three sons wanted to sort out our own selves – to be accepted and recognised for what we do.

I think that was an achievement for all of us to manage and I think Mirka and Georges had a huge role in that, because they were always completely supportive.

I am still in awe of the way she keeps going. She is seriously independent and always will be, but she's not a spring chicken any more – age is catching up on her a little bit.

She complains about getting older and memory and mobility and stuff like that but she's still got that really beautiful energy and I can't get enough of it. When we catch up, we take up from where we left off. There's no distance there at all because we're back to where we were. It's been like that for a long time.

The two main things I learned from Mirka?

One is live life to the max – make the most of every day. The other is to be generous. Generous to people, generous to the world and your community, and generous to yourself, too.

I think that one other basic thing I learned is just to love art and believe in art and what art can do to people – whether to entertain or make people laugh or just make them feel anything. Mirka did bring joy to people with her paintings. That makes me so proud of her.

These days, I come down to Melbourne and we have lunch together and because she's conscious of time being finite in the human experience, she comes up with great memories to talk about and so she'll spend time going over things about my childhood. There are things she tells me about watching me grow up that she remembers with such beautiful clarity – insights of what Georges was like when I was a little kid and how much he adored me. It's very comforting stuff and I don't have to prod or question – she just comes out with all of it. I don't think I have any mysteries. I think we've covered a lot of it and yet she keeps coming up with more stuff – she's making a real effort to give it to me each time we are together. When I leave Melbourne to drive back home to my own family, there's a sadness because, you know, these lunches are not going to go on forever.

It's not just about the past. We cover the future things too. She adores my daughter and she'll tell me how lucky I am to have a beautiful child like that. Then she says how Audrey is so lucky to have a wonderful father, and encourages me to be a great father to her, always. It's a transition – her reminding me it's my duty to make sure I am a good parent and how important that responsibility is.

I think my daughter understands it's okay to be an individual. Mirka instilled that in me and, whether it was by design or circumstance, she imbued me with resilience – and the profound importance of self-expression, even if it's just good for the soul.

You know what? Boy, I *was* lucky to have Mirka as my mother.

GERALDINE COX

Geraldine Cox's love of travel and human rights began while working in the Department of Foreign Affairs, and she is the only Australian to have been granted Cambodian citizenship by royal decree. Geraldine is the first to admit that her mum used to view her as wayward and a troublemaker. Her life as the founder of Sunrise Cambodia – a home for children – and her official honour as a Member of the Order in Australia in 2000 are achievements her mum never would have predicted.

Mum had a little girl – Leonie – and she died in a tragic accident when the safety pin on the ribbon on her dummy was put in her mouth the wrong way around and she choked on it. My mother never, ever recovered from this loss.

She tortured herself by saying that she had murdered her daughter and she had a serious nervous breakdown before I was born, so the doctor told Dad that the only thing that might shake her out of it was to have another child.

Pictured: Dorothy Cox and Geraldine Cox

Then I was born.

Mum went off the deep end straight away, because when I was born I looked the image of Leonie and she thought that Leonie had come back to punish her. Much later in her life she used to joke that there was a bit of truth in that. She'd had shock treatment before I was born and she had shock treatment regularly, right up until the last year of her life when she was ninety-five. The shock treatment really seemed to work with my mother. She would enter a depressed state where she couldn't function very well and got no joy out of life at all, and then she would go on a course of shock treatment and she'd be fine.

I was the fourth daughter of a milkman in the suburbs of Adelaide. Mum was basically a homemaker. Dad was a Victorian type of man who didn't show any affection – we never doubted that we were loved, he just couldn't show it. It flowed through to my mother too, but her love was evident in other things that she did for us – making our clothes, cooking beautiful food. It was a safe and secure home life.

Mum didn't have a big education and neither did my father, so they weren't the sort of people you could sit around and talk with for hours.

It didn't help that I was a really difficult teenager. I was wilful, I didn't obey anything – just very difficult to handle.

When I was about fifteen I'd go to bed, kiss Mum and Dad goodnight and wait until they'd gone to sleep. Then, at ten o'clock, I would sneak out and catch a taxi and go and meet whoever was the man of the moment. I had a very high sex drive.

Around that age, I was going out with a Yugoslav refugee

from the Red Cross camp and I thought he was the most exotic thing on two legs. He had an accent and a walk, European suits – he was just completely irresistible. He was twenty-one and he had no idea that I was underage, and he didn't understand the laws of Australia – as far as that was concerned, anyway.

I was so enamoured with him, I would take days off work and ask girlfriends to ring up the office and pretend to be my mother saying: 'Oh, it's Mrs Cox here – Geraldine's got a migraine she won't be in today.' To cover myself, I used to tell Mum that we were not allowed to receive personal phone calls at work.

I would spend all day with this man and come home for tea in the evening. They must have smelt a rat because one day, Mum did call – she said it was an emergency and asked to be put through. It might have been an emergency for all I knew – maybe the house caught fire, I don't know – but she rang up and they said: 'Oh, I'm sorry, but you rang earlier today to say Geraldine won't be in.'

Mum was furious. When I came home she would not stop raving about it: 'We know what you have been doing, you wait till your father comes home and I will tell him all about it.'

She was just bluffing, but I didn't know that. I said: 'I don't care what you do – I love him, I will marry him,' and she said: 'Marry who?' Then it all came out. I was pretty much barred from that relationship after that – I had to really, really go to great lengths to see him, but it wasn't a relationship that was ever going to end well.

Mum found it repugnant that her fifteen-year-old was having sex in those days – and so did my father. They were ashamed of me. I was of the opinion, even without knowing much about the world, that what I was doing was natural and healthy and it wasn't hurting anybody. I have always had a healthy regard for sex as a pleasure that we are all entitled to have. But Mum didn't share that opinion back then.

Mum was lucky to get a kiss on the cheek from Dad for Mother's Day and Christmas, and I never saw them hold hands or hug or do anything affectionate – ever. Dad was not a philanderer or anything like that – I'm sure he treated Mum with the utmost respect. I just think they both had a low sex drive and that it was a part of their life that didn't really affect them very much. Mum was convinced that the purpose of sex was just to have children, and she even believed that once you had sex you conceived straight away – she was not very sexually aware. That was how I was brought up and my two sisters weren't too impressed with me either – they were both virgins when they got married. None of my family could understand why I thought so much of sex.

When I was in my early twenties I met a Greek man who was one of the loves of my life. Mum was in the local grocery shop one day and a neighbour said to Mum: 'Oh Dot, you must be so upset that Geraldine is going out with that Greek!' Mum put her potatoes and onions in her bag and turned around and said: 'I don't know, if it is good enough for the Queen of England, it is good enough for our Geraldine.'

She didn't really feel that way but she was never going to let the neighbours know that that she didn't approve. She was loyal to us – even when she disagreed.

We were going to get married. He sent me off for tests to see if I could have children because we'd had a pretty open love affair – we never used condoms. Sure enough it was proven that I couldn't conceive.

When he dumped me, it had a really bad effect. I decided to join the Department of Foreign Affairs because I thought: 'Well, if I can't be a wife and mother, I'll live a life of glamour. I'll travel and swan around in a black cocktail dress and get seduced by James Bond-type men.'

That wasn't exactly how it turned out.

I never really confided in Mum. When I was going into hospital to have these tests to see if I could have children, I was pretty distressed about the results but I never told her how bad it made me feel. She would have said something like: 'Well, that's what happens to girls who have sex,' and she made me feel like it was a just punishment – that I deserved it in some way. Her attitude didn't particularly hurt me because I didn't believe it – but it did make me realise I could not talk to her about everything I felt or did.

Any time I brought a new suitable boy home she would say, after the third date: 'Oh, do you think you could marry him?' I would have only met him three times but she was hoping for me to get married and settle down so that she could stop worrying.

Dad died of lung cancer when he was sixty-nine after a long stint in the nursing home. Mum couldn't handle his deteriorating health – he was incontinent and the whole house just smelled.

It was taking its toll on Mum too – she was actually having a nervous breakdown at the time that he died. There she was in the psychiatric clinic having electric shocks and Dad was dying a slow and horrible death in the nursing home, without her.

It was a great sadness for me – I felt torn between my mum and dad – and then when he did die, she wasn't in a position to really understand what had happened. We took her to the funeral because the doctor said that it was really important for her to see her husband in an open casket so she could accept that he was gone. Shortly after all that, I had to go to Iran on a posting with the embassy. I couldn't be there to spend time with her when she needed me.

I took long service leave not long after because I could tell she was not right after Dad's passing. She had a little unit in town and I stayed there with her. One day she said to me: 'Don't wake me up in the morning; I want to sleep in. Don't wake me up.'

So that night she took a whole bottle of scotch and sleeping pills together – and she wasn't a drinker. She had written a note to apologise to everybody and tried to kill herself in the night.

Of course, I didn't know this was happening at the time. A girlfriend rang me on the home number while I was trying to enjoy the sleep-in myself, and the phone kept on ringing and ringing and ringing. I thought: 'Fudge, Mum – pick up the bloody phone.' But it just kept ringing.

Eventually, I went to the phone in her bedroom and I could see she was breathing in a very laboured way, and drooling too, and there was the note and the bottle – everything was all on the bed. There was no doubt that she was trying to kill herself, so I dropped the phone like a mad woman and I ran naked into the next-door neighbour's house just saying: 'Help, help, help – I don't know how to call an ambulance,' because I didn't. I'd been living overseas for so long that I couldn't remember. The poor fellow next door was sitting down with his family and two kids at the table for breakfast when this mad, naked woman they hadn't even met yet came racing in.

They called an ambulance, which came very quickly. Mum was in intensive care for about six weeks, and because it was a suicide attempt she had to have more psychiatric treatment, too.

I wasn't angry at all. She was getting no joy out of life – she didn't want to eat anything, she didn't watch anything. I did kind of understand why she was pushed to it and I never blamed her or criticised her for what she did. I knew it wasn't my fault. She was just so unhappy.

I didn't know it at the time but, in retrospect, I saw it as an opportunity to show my mother that I really did love her. With everything being how it was when I was younger, I didn't come to that realisation until much later in my life. Losing Leonie had been such a massive thing for her. My attitude used to be: 'Lots of families lose somebody, so get over this,' and I was a bit impatient with her for not being able to resolve the grief.

I saw her as someone who was led by whatever happened to her in life. She was not able to rise up and overcome any difficulties – she just gave into them. It made me pity her for not being able to be the master of her own life. She was the victim of whatever circumstance was to befall her.

Later in my life, I told a story in my own book about when I adopted my daughter Lisa, who was mentally and physically challenged. I was so affected by this that when I couldn't see a light at the end of the tunnel, I thought about killing both her and myself together. For one night, I felt myself weaken and I planned to take her with me. I didn't think, at the time, that I was doing what my mother did – it never occurred to me. I bought us matching nighties, I got a bottle of French champagne, I had my hair done and had full make-up on, all because I thought I wanted to look gorgeous when they found me in the morning. I had it all planned. I was about to give Lisa the sleeping pills and I was going to take the second lot for myself once I knew she was asleep. But then she looked up at me. I struggled to make eye contact with her in those days – her eyes were always going around all over the place. She was very autistic and she couldn't really understand that eye contact was a form of communication. So, for the first time, I had this eye communication with her for about two seconds and she looked at me with what I perceived to be a look of love and trust. I burst into tears and I thought: 'Well, I have the right to take my own life but not hers – no matter what.' Motherhood is a huge responsibility.

I was thirty-two years old and Lisa was seven at that time. I'd adopted her because I couldn't have my own children but her illness was beyond what I could cope with. I found a place in Adelaide where she could go into care – the most difficult day I've ever had was the day I had to relinquish her.

I still have pain when I think about it. She had the most beautiful long, curly hair down to her waist – it was my pride and joy. But the authorities she was going to stay with said that they couldn't possibly handle her hair and they told me that I had to cut it. I remember washing it and then having to cut it off. I put it in a silver box that I still have today in the house and I pack with me wherever I go. Although Lisa hadn't died, in many ways I felt as though I'd lost her, so that was when I started to understand a bit better about what Mum went through when her own little daughter was taken away from her.

I will be always grateful to my sister, Sandra, because she did everything to help my mother when I was working overseas. She had her garage converted into a sweet little granny flat and the whole family – her two children and her husband – were terribly open and loving and they just included Mum in their daily life when I couldn't be there.

Mum lived with them when she came out of the hospital and she started to be more sociable – a big change from all those years with Dad. She even met a man, Jack, when she was seventy-six – she was madly in love and they got married. She had this whole second go at life, which was amazing because when she married my father, life was certainly not all romance.

I loved him as much as I did my own dad – and he was wonderful to my mother. They would go to fancy dress balls, go jazz dancing twice a week – he was just what my mother needed and what she should have had when she was younger. She loved the life she created with Jack – they were together for about twelve years. What that taught me is that it is never too late to have a relationship – even if you are not looking for it. It wasn't until she had been married to Jack and I came home on a holiday that she said to me: 'I can understand now why you were so difficult to control when you were younger because with Jack I have had' – I'll never forget what she called it – 'my first organism.'

I didn't correct her – how could I when she had confided

her innermost secret? After she'd told me, I think we both collapsed into peals of laughter and just about wet ourselves at the kitchen sink. It was a really poignant time between the two of us when she was saying to me that now she understood.

Her whole personality changed with this new man. Mum was always a glamorous woman and Dad never appreciated her or even expressed his pleasure at how she looked. But Jack wanted to show her off all the time and was obviously so proud of her. Mum really loved being made to feel special like that and it made me feel good to see her happy in that way – embracing this part of herself that had been so buried all her life.

I know they were having sex well into Mum's eighties because I would stay with them when I came home and it was obvious what they were up to. I thought: 'This is bloody marvellous – I have this to look forward to in my old age.'

When Mum was in her eighties and Jack died, she went into a nursing home and I went home to visit her. My kids at the orphanage in Cambodia said: 'Why doesn't she come here?' and I explained what a nursing home was – this place you send your parents when you can't take care of them. They were horrified.

They said: 'You should be home taking care of your mother,' and I said: 'Well, I can't be in two places at one time – I am either here with you or at home with my mother.' They decided they would rather I stay with them of course, but they were still very critical.

When I visited her there, I used to take her out in a wheelchair because it was a long way to walk to the car, and as I'd wheel her past the recreation room where the other old people were, she'd say to them: 'I am going home with my daughter for a holiday,' and you could tell she was really thrilled about coming home with me.

We always stayed at my girlfriend's house and we slept together in the same big bed. She said to me one morning: 'You snore,' and I said: 'Well, you fart,' and we both sat around laughing.

I used to get her up in the morning and we would have a shower together just to make sure that she didn't fall over or anything like that. You can imagine – in those days, I was more than a hundred kilos and she was a tiny little thing and we would both be in the shower together. Afterwards I'd sit her on the toilet seat and I'd powder her all over. She really loved being pampered, and I was happy to do it. That was the closest we had ever been.

She had a bout of neck cancer and when the doctor told her, she asked what the prognosis was.

He said: 'Well, you can have radiation.'

'How much longer would that give me?' she asked.

'About six months.'

Mum said, 'I'll take it.' She loved life enough to want to fight. But after those six months, the doctor told her the cancer had come back. She didn't want any more radiation then. She made all these decisions by herself.

Towards the end, I was there, talking to her all the time because I had read somewhere that when you're in a coma or dying the last sense you lose is your sense of hearing.

When she was near the end, I whispered to her: 'Mum, please don't die today – it's April Fool's Day, so please hang on for another day.' And she did.

You're never really prepared to lose your mother. It was early in the morning and I was watching her breathing – it was very laboured. She breathed in and out, in and out and then she breathed in and then there was nothing out – I knew that she was gone.

The undertakers came and I said: 'She wants an open casket but in my opinion she looks horrible.' I didn't think it would be respectful of me to let people see her like that. The funeral director said: 'Don't you worry about that, give us two days and come back and have a look at her before the funeral. You can make up your mind then whether you want the open casket or not.'

They did an amazing job. She had everything done and I went to look at her and I tell you, she never looked so good in her whole life.

She had mascara, she had blue eyeshadow, she had her nails done and she looked fabulous, really fabulous. After the funeral, I went to the funeral director's office to pay the bill and I said: 'Can I drop off and have my face done?'

Mum's funeral was standing room only and half the staff came from the nursing home because she was loved so much there. Six of my Cambodian students were studying at Adelaide University at the time and they all came too. That was the first time I really realised how popular my mother was with people and it was heartwarming.

She was almost ninety-five when she died three years ago. She had the cover of my book posted on the back of her door in her room at the nursing home so that when she was in bed she could look at it, and every time the carers would come in her room, she'd say: 'That's my daughter, up there.' In the end, she was very proud of me.

Losing Mum really showed me how much my children in Cambodia have lost and it made me feel more grateful for the kind of life and relationship with my mother that I had. It hasn't changed the way I treat them – I have always loved them with all my heart – but it helps me understand more what they've lost.

On the second of April each year, I light an incense stick in my little spirit house and go out in the moonlight. I also light a candle and pray, and then, inside, I light another candle and let it go all the way down till there's nothing left. That's my tribute to Mum.

BENJAMIN LAW

As a writer, Benjamin Law is a regular contributor
to a variety of publications, including a weekly
column in Fairfax's *Good Weekend*. His memoir, *The
Family Law*, was shortlisted in the Australian Book
Industry Awards for Book of the Year in 2011 and
has been adapted into a TV show for SBS. He's the
kind of guy who loves sharing a good story – even
if it means revealing some personal details. And
his mum doesn't seem to mind. Benjamin admits
that the relationship between him and his mother
may be closer than most. Are they the world's
only mother and son sex advice columnists? It's a
reasonable assumption...

I was seventeen when I came out as gay to Mum. I'd already told
my best friend, Rebecca, and that gave me a bit of forward
momentum to be able to tell my mum because I knew that she
was the second person I wanted to tell. It was scary. I had that
whole: 'Mum I have something I need to tell you,' and I was

Pictured: Jenny Law and Benjamin Law

crying so much that I couldn't even get it out, which, of course, would freak any parent out.

She was like: 'What is wrong?' And because I couldn't get it out, she started playing a guessing game.

'Are you on drugs?'

'No.'

'Have you gotten Rebecca pregnant?'

'No.'

And I'm thinking to myself: 'You're definitely getting colder.'

'Are you gay?'

'Yes.'

Her shoulders slumped in relief and sympathy, and she patted my back and said: 'Don't be silly, there's nothing wrong with being gay – it just means that something went wrong in the womb, that's all.'

I think that response is so hilarious in retrospect because she's comforting and reassuring me, while also basically telling me I'm deformed in some way. You know: 'You don't need to blame yourself – it's just that my womb malfunctioned...'

It was her way of saying: 'Look – it's a glitch in the natural order of things,' – and in a way it is, just as left-handedness is. It's nobody's fault, it's just how people come out. And that's what she was trying to communicate with me in a very roundabout way.

I don't think I could have continued having an honest relationship about my life and my friendship circles with my mum if that conversation hadn't happened.

I'm one of many siblings. There are five of us. Amongst my mum's generation, a family that size isn't unusual, but on the Sunshine Coast growing up in the eighties and nineties we were definitely the biggest family at our school. And I'm smashed right in the middle – the meat in the sandwich. And I'm happy to be the meat in the sandwich because that's the part that everyone enjoys, right?

I was born in 1982. There was my older brother, Andrew, and our eldest sister, Candy, who'd come before me, then four years after me Tammy, my sister, was born, then Michelle.

I'm at the age now that all my friends are popping out their first and sometimes second babies, and you see the pressures up close – what's involved in parenthood first-hand – so I asked my mum: 'How did you have five? And why did you have five?'

And she said: 'Your Dad and I just never had that conversation.'

I guess that shows the extent of their communication skills with each other, which is probably why they got divorced when I was twelve years old. I guess the other explanation is, my Mum just loved being a mum – she loves being a mum still. She always loved having kids in her life – whatever the ups and downs in her marriage, she thought we were wonderful and adorable, and she thought we were really cute. We seemed to really cheer her up. For my father, I think he always wanted a big family – there's some prestige and status in having a big family, especially when you come from China. He was the only child of his family – that was pre-one-child policy.

My parents met in Hong Kong in the early 1970s and they got married super quickly, after only a few months of knowing each other. Dad knew that he didn't want to live in Hong Kong.

He wanted to live in a place where there was opportunity and room to raise a family. Hong Kong has neither of those things. Hong Kong has great shopping, but it also has claustrophobia – so they moved to Australia and set up shop. One of the reasons they moved to Australia was that my dad knew some people in Queensland already in the restaurant trade.

My mum, on the other hand, had never been to Australia. As an adult, I think back on what a huge gamble she took in trusting a man she didn't even know that well to go to a country she'd never visited – where she had no friends, no family members – to start a new life. I think that was very brave.

The restaurant business, as anyone who's worked in it would know, is pretty brutal. They were both working seven days and nights a week.

When her first child came, she kept working, and when Andrew was born things got busier, but they still worked at a Chinese takeaway restaurant called Sunny Village in Caloundra. When I was born, I created a bit of a rift between my parents, because Mum just knew immediately – with three kids, very young children with only three years between them, it would be unsustainable for her to keep working at the restaurant, and if my father wanted to have a family with three kids, part of the deal was that she wasn't going to work any more.

Apparently Dad was pretty angry about that, but Mum – all credit to her – was very steadfast and firm that she wasn't setting foot back in the restaurant. She was going to raise the three kids full-time at home.

I got the full force of my mother's love from day one. I had a fantastic childhood – the teen years weren't so happy but childhood was really fantastic. As a young child, you're born into this ready-made ecosystem of love and affection – you've got your natural allies there in your siblings and because my mum wasn't working outside the home, I was very well taken care of.

I was a very low-maintenance child, she says. She could plonk me in front of the television or with some books and milk and I'd be very, very happy, so she could wrangle Candy and Andrew from getting into fights. It was a house of great affection and love and she provided that – she was at the heart of it.

There's that cliché that the younger child gets it easy and in my case that's definitely true. I think with Candy and Andrew, she was very protective – being a mother for the first time in a new country added to that – but with me, she knew the ropes, so I think I got that sense of leniency and adventure.

I was such an attention hog – even then I was seeking the limelight. I totally embraced the fact that I was the youngest child at that stage, the fact that I had a bit of novelty value – and they completely gave it to me. As much as I was a low-maintenance child, I was very rude and cheeky and as soon as I could talk, I was saying rude and disgusting things. I think everyone found their place very quickly.

Reading came to me naturally and I think a lot of it had to do with my mum, partly because I always remembered there being a lot of books in the house. My parents themselves aren't huge readers but they always had a lot of kids' books – for them, books were never a waste of money. That whole thing about Chinese parents and the emphasis they place on education is very real and certainly was in my family. One of my happiest memories is being snuggled up in Mum's bed – I'd snuggle into the pillow with her and we'd read the books together.

She was very sentimental. She had big old cassettes and a dictaphone that she probably bought from Brashs or something, and cassettes of us reading are still in the house somewhere now, I think. Even then, she knew that those memories would be very precious to her. Looking back, it made me feel very special that this seemingly ordinary moment was something worth recording. She was recording us because we were the most precious, interesting, fascinating things in her life, so video cameras, dictaphones, cameras – they were all there.

When I ask her whether she had ambitions outside of motherhood she has different ways of responding. She always wanted to be a mum and I think that's something that's not appreciated enough these days – that, for some people, motherhood is the ultimate. For her, it certainly was. Partly that's a generational thing and partly that's a cultural thing. She realises she is very much the product of her own circumstances – she says she would have also probably made a good nurse.

Her eldest sister, Josephine, was a nurse and I think my mum admired that because part of Mum's family story is that the eldest sister supported their huge family. My mum is one of seven children, but her oldest sister supported the family for a really long time when they were having trouble in Hong Kong.

While Mum admires Josephine for what she did, she can't stand the sight of blood. She was fine fixing up our scrapes and that sort of stuff but she was like: 'I was happy dealing with your blood and poo growing up, but I'm not sure how well I'd go dealing with other people's blood and poo.'

Looking at the job I have as a writer and journalist – my sister is a writer, too – it might have been influenced by the fact that Mum's a really good conversationalist and raconteur and she's very curious about people. I think those are two qualities that are vital in writing human stories and writing real stories. She sometime speculates that she would've liked to have been a journalist or a writer of some sort – and I think she would make a good one. But, really, she did fulfil her own ambition, which was to be a mum – and a really good one at that.

My mum recently had her sixtieth birthday and after we toasted, I asked everyone at the table to name something that they inherited from her. We all said we inherited her skin. She has very good skin – she looks twenty years younger than she is. In terms of other things I inherited from her, one would be a deep sense of sentimentality. I'm such a sook. Mum's a bit of a hoarder. She finds it very difficult to let go of things – especially things from our childhood – and for a long time I was like that too. I'm very conscious of the fact that I'll hold onto things as a keepsake or a souvenir, when it's like, Ben, you really don't need that in your life.

Definitely life with Mum is a big, loud gabfest. My mum is like a shark – sharks will die if they stop swimming, and my mum will die if she stops talking. We sometimes share hotel rooms when we're travelling together and I'll just be slowly waking up but she's talking from the moment she's conscious. Once I'm awake, I tend to like talking quite a bit, too.

As for nature vs. nurture, it's very hard to differentiate the two because for me those things in our household were just so close in a way. I know I got some things from my father – I look exactly like my dad. I think there are some values they instilled in us that I'm pretty sure I wouldn't have if I was raised by anyone else.

Five kids is a pretty big troupe – it's almost like a science experiment, in a way. You've got these five kids and you've got these extremely different personality types, but the things that unify us I think we must have absorbed from our parents – one is a deep value of education.

They weren't tiger parents by any means – they never said: 'Be an accountant, be a doctor, be a lawyer.' But it was a huge thing to be able to go to a good school and to learn, and that's something a lot of my friends didn't have because their parents were more relaxed about that ratio between leisure and work time.

From both of my parents I inherited a strong work ethic. My mum was always of the belief that if you committed to something, you had to see it through, and I've always felt that myself. I think a lot of it is witnessing what your parents do in their own lives – it's not even them sitting you down for a lesson.

My parents split up when I was twelve and they had a really protracted divorce arrangement – they weren't even divorced by the time I was seventeen.

So, my high school experience was pretty miserable and I was often the middleman. Divorce is an interesting thing. It's a situation that can compel adults to start behaving like children. I mean, I love my parents but I think all adults are capable of behaving like children, and during the divorce proceedings they definitely were like that. They weren't talking to each other – they were so furious with each other they could only communicate through intermediaries and I was one of the primary ones. I really resented that.

Sometimes, some of the siblings would stay with Dad

more, and it broke Mum's heart that her children were being separated from her and each other.

When you've got a parent who's not coping and you normally rely on them, you can lash out. That was me. I think Mum paints a rosier picture – she says I was actually quite good during this period – but I remember saying some pretty awful things to her, telling her to her face to basically get her act together. Whereas, in that moment and in that period, I think it's very difficult for anyone to get their act together. That pressure of parenthood, combined with your own personal challenges of divorce, is pretty wearing.

I think we've got a really great relationship now. One of the breakthroughs was when she discovered text messaging. I don't know what it is about my brain wiring but I'm a text-based person – emails, texts. I've never been that fond of phone calls.

Mum was really frustrated by that because she wasn't that confident using new technology. We tried teaching her how to use a computer for a very long time but the breakthrough was actually getting an iPhone – finally, she could actually touch things on a screen and she loved it, so now we've got this really fantastic text messaging relationship. She's fluent in emoji – she's far more fluent than I am. It sort of feels like teenage exchanges with each other. A bit of gossip comes through – I show the text to my boyfriend and it's like deciphering hieroglyphics, but she's so expressive through these emojis and pictures. Her favourites are the poo emoji, the dancing senorita emoji, the delicious emoji, where the smiley face is licking his lips – it's just very, very funny.

I wrote a book about my family that came out in 2010, called *The Family Law*. Everyone assumes that writing a memoir is easy – you know the story of your life and your family's life. The truth is it's very difficult because you realise that there are huge gaps in your understanding of your family story, and to go about it professionally and interview your parents and ask questions you hadn't thought to ask them simply as their child reveals all these histories and truths that make you extend huge reserves of sympathy and empathy for the lives that they've led. I think that was a real turning point. I always thought that my mum was strong but, writing that book, I realised what a hero she was.

When we went to New Zealand to celebrate my mum's sixtieth, no partners chose to come with us, I think because they knew better. It was the first time all five kids had been together like that with Mum – probably since we were children. Part of me was dreading it because I could just see disaster happening. Even though we love each other and we get along great, I think any time with any family can end up pretty fractious if you're in a contained space with them – but I think age has mellowed us.

I found all of us willing to be very accommodating with each other. We're just in the process of moving Mum out of our childhood home, too, which sounds like a sad thing – and in some ways it is – but it's Mum turning a new page. She's really thrilled, excited, nervous and giddy about the prospect of moving from the family home in the Sunshine Coast to a new place in Brisbane to be close to where most of her kids live now. I think there's a sense of optimism. It's really improved everyone's mood.

She loves my boyfriend, Scott – we knew each other as friends in high school, but we didn't get together until we were at university, so she already was a bit familiar with him.

Gays don't really date, they just hook up and take it from there, really. So, in a way, Mum and Scott had a date before he and I did. She wanted to know more about him, so they went to the local Sizzler restaurant and it was adorable. She thinks he's great and Scott's been such a rock for my mum in so many ways. She calls him her other son and I have to remind her: 'You've actually got two sons already, Mum,' but he's another one. Scott's very good at providing emotional support for her – because she's known him for such a long time, there's inherent trust there. Sometimes Scott's having a moment with his mum and I'm having a moment with my mum and we're just like: 'Do we just want to swap – how about I talk to your mum for a while and help her out and you talk to my mum?' That's actually quite handy.

Both of my parents, but especially my mum, always told us: 'Make sure you're doing something you like, make sure you're good at it and make sure you can earn money from it.' All the kids have ended up doing something they wanted to do – so it was really fantastic that they instilled that in us.

A lot of my writing is about my family – and a lot of my writing features her as well. She embraces that – in fact she's been onstage with me at festivals talking about it and I think that writing, for me, has been an important way of reconciling with my family and my family history. She feels that, for a long time, she was the least heard voice in the family, which is funny because she's very much heard, by virtue of her talking a lot. But being able to present her story to a wider audience has been a very satisfying thing for her. I'm not one of those people who's going to write something and put it out there only for her to discover it later – it really matters what she thinks about my writing.

We've turned *The Family Law* into a TV show on SBS, which aired in early 2016. As strange and surreal as that experience was – we're getting actors to play versions of us on television – for my mum and all my family members, seeing that version of our lives being put on screen was kind of affirming.

Mum and I write a sex and relationships advice column together for *The Lifted Brow* – a literary journal out of Melbourne – so people send us really revolting personal questions and Jenny goes first and Benjamin goes second. That's pretty special – and unusual.

The questions we get are all uncomfortable – I mean, they're talking about vibrators and masturbation and threesomes and polyamory – but my mum is so open and curious and fascinated by other people, and especially about sex. A lot of people are so shocked that a mum and her children would talk about things like that so frankly, but that's always been the case for me growing up.

She used to say when we were growing up: 'No ring – no ding,' which basically meant no sex before marriage, but now, considering how terribly her marriage ended, she has more of a 'try before you buy' belief system.

Mum is a big lover and almost patron of the arts in a way – she loves anything that really stimulates her artistically or culturally. She's a creative girl at heart herself, I think.

I think my mum loves to travel as much as she loves the arts. She's got a school reunion in Malaysia and she needs company with her – she hasn't got a partner – so we're going to go to that. I love spending time with her because, even now that I'm an adult, she has so much to teach me. For example, when I'm moisturising my face, I just kind of slather moisturiser on my face – you know it's just cream – and she's always telling me: 'You've got to just moisturise with your ring and pinkie fingers because that applies the least pressure on your face.'

One of things I sometimes think about – it's slightly odd – is I wonder what would it have been like to know my parents at the same age as I am now? Would we have been friends? Would we have gotten along? It's a wistful exercise, I think, and to see these other women at the reunion who know a version of Mum that I don't will be really interesting. I'll have a lot of questions.

Mum and I went on a road trip together a while back. I had a work commitment in Alice Springs and I thought: 'I should take my mum, she's always wanted to see Uluru.' We only had one major fight, which is a pretty good strike rate for us. One of her favourite things about the trip was being able to pee in the desert. She loved peeing out in the open.

I can't fake anything in front of her. Mum knows me in many, many profound ways. I think it's really comforting – for some people their greatest endeavour is to be known, for people to understand them. I think that because of my mum, I've had that from a really young age.

LYNN GILMARTIN

Lynn Gilmartin was a toddler when she came to
Australia with her family as an Irish immigrant.
Her career in marketing at one of Australia's leading
casinos led to a hosting role on local TV, and now
she lives in Los Angeles where she is the anchor
of *World Poker Tour* on Fox Sports. For Lynn,
her mum's commitment to spiritual learning and
positivity have been pivotal in guiding her ability
to recognise and accept all the opportunities that
come her way.

I was born in Dublin, Ireland in 1984. In 1986 my family
moved to Australia, which seemed to be the thing to do for
many Europeans in the eighties. My father was offered a great
business opportunity, so off we went.

My mother always had a part-time job while my brother,
who is seven years older than me, and I, were at school. When
I was in primary school, Mum got a job as a sales consultant
for a cosmetics company. Prior to this, she never really wore

Pictured: Lynn Gilmartin and Maura McCarthy Gilmartin

make-up. Suddenly she found herself in this wonderful world of creativity, and make-up artistry became a big part of her life. As a kid I'd always be playing with her palettes of shadows and lipsticks. She'd have drawers and cupboards overflowing with cosmetics. I'd often be her model at home to test new products or techniques on. All those lessons have come in quite handy now!

Make-up became her own creative expression. She loves to always look her best, which makes her feel her best, so you'll very rarely see my mum not made up perfectly. While I have a bit of a barefoot-loving side, I have adopted her enjoyment of seeing myself as my own canvas. It's another beautiful way of embracing our creativity and treating our lives as works of art.

Growing up, I'd always hear my mother listening to cassette tapes of audio books and lectures in the bathroom as she did her make-up each morning. She still does this, and now so do I. She'd listen to all kinds of New Age authors, such as Louise Hay, Carolyn Myss, Wayne Dyer and Abraham Hicks, sharing their philosophies on self-love and living a fulfilling life. These philosophies have played a major role in the most important lessons my mother has taught me.

While I wasn't often actively listening as a child – and throughout my awkward teens I probably rejected a lot of it – growing up surrounded by all kinds of personal-growth and love-filled wisdom set a strong foundation in me of self-awareness and taking responsibility for my own life and happiness. My mother taught me to nurture myself with love, which then enables me to share that love with others.

My mother's love of the self-development aisle of the

bookstore stemmed from quite an ordeal she went through in the early eighties, when she was in an accident that caused a small haemorrhage in her spinal cord. This was before I was born, and she was in no physical condition to carry a baby, but when she fell pregnant not long afterwards, she persisted through it. She suffered from so much pain throughout my younger years. She developed all kinds of severe allergies and saw countless doctors to try and help her, but without much success. It was when she discovered alternative medicine that she truly began to heal, and that is what triggered her passion for learning about the mind–body connection and various kinds of esoteric teachings.

One subject she was really drawn to was astrology, and she's been studying it now for about twenty years. For her, it opened up a whole new understanding of herself and of others. Our family and all of my mum's friends (and my friends!) are always turning to Mum for advice from their charts. She's like an oracle. It's hilarious how many times my friends have said to me: 'Can you ask your mum what is going on in my chart right now?' Astrology has really unleashed her true gift of helping others.

Astrology is just not the horoscopes you see in the newspaper. It's much, much deeper and more specific than that. Mum will often blow me away with how specific her readings can be. It's mostly about having an awareness of our emotions and how they're affected each day by the alignment of the solar system.

Mum has given my entire family so much priceless guidance throughout our lives. Once she began her journey of personal growth, we all followed suit and went on journeys of our own. As a kid, I remember seeing Mum and Dad go to seminars and bookstores together, and while mum began studying astrology, my dad studied reiki and reflexology. I feel so lucky to have such awesome parents.

I'm not from a family of performers, so I'm not sure where this desire came from, but I've always had a deep love of performing. 'I want to be an actress!' It was something I used to declare often, as a child. My parents have always supported this dream, or any dream my brother and I have had. Mum would drive me to all kinds of acting and dance classes. I started them when I was around five years old. If I wasn't hiding in my room with the family's video recorder filming fake news reports or rehearsing for my primary school's play, I'd be choreographing dance routines in my neighbour's garage to *The Immaculate Collection* by Madonna. I simply loved putting on a show.

I was a very determined young girl, and meticulously organised when it came to my career. In my later years of primary school, I kept a folder with my resume and headshots which I'd organised myself, photocopies of acting agents' contact details and all kinds of auditioning advice I'd sourced from my classes. My mum never had to organise a thing. I'd pretty much just say, 'This is what I want to do, this is where I have to go and this is how it has to be done. Can you help me make it happen?' So off we'd go. My mum always made me believe I could create whatever I wanted to create in my life.

When I was about twelve, however, I lost a lot of confidence and things began to change dramatically. I went through hell with bad friendships and bullying at school, and to top it all off I fell over on stage in the middle of a show and was mortified.

It was then that I decided to quit acting and focus on my high school studies and getting a 'real career'. I continued to dabble in dancing and modelling throughout high school, but I had given acting the flick.

During the years of issues with friends, I'd constantly suffer from nosebleeds. A doctor wanted to burn off some vein or vessel in my nose to treat it, but my mum knew it was an emotional trigger and was determined to help me break it. Inspired by Louise Hay, she'd have me repeat the mantra 'I approve of myself' in my head continuously when I felt a nosebleed coming. She was always trying to show me the light within myself and that I didn't need the approval of the other girls at school to feel worthy. I remember she would say to me: 'You need to love yourself,' but I wouldn't quite get it. It wasn't until I was in my twenties that her messages all became crystal clear to me.

As my confidence grew stronger and I got a new group of friends in high school, my nosebleeds miraculously stopped. Even now, a couple of times per year or so when I'm having an emotional moment of weakness, a nosebleed will come, and every time it happens, it's when my self-esteem has taken a beating. To this day, whenever that happens, I sit in the bathroom with a tissue to my nose repeating: 'I approve of myself, I approve of myself.'

I don't believe any child can be fully protected from emotional pain growing up. It's all part of the human process, contributing to our personal growth as well as to our understanding of others and ourselves. My mum still reminds me that we always need to experience contrast to fully appreciate and recognise what it is that we want. If we don't understand what we don't want, then how do we know what we do want? While my mum instilled such strong values in me, I still had to go through a period of tough times. Experiencing rejection and lack of self-confidence has allowed all my mum's teachings to set in deeply as I've grown into adulthood. I do need to love myself. I do need to approve of myself. Because depending on other people for their love and approval will never fill that empty void within if I don't.

If I were to recall a quote of my mother's that I've heard the most, it would be: 'Always do the best for yourself.'

I was a really focused student at high school, and I went on to get a diploma in public relations and a degree in marketing. My meticulous self-organisation with my career continued and I always got myself a job. When I was at university, I'd work in my field full-time between semesters, so I graduated with loads of experience.

After completing my studies, I pursued my marketing career and secured a fantastic job at a casino, which I thrived in. I loved that a large part of my job was planning events, which constantly reminded me of my passion for performing. After three years and receiving a huge promotion at work, another opportunity came up: I could quit my secure corporate career to hop on a flight to Las Vegas to work with an online channel, reporting on the *World Series of Poker*, and then continue around the world to other major poker tournaments. I wasn't a presenter or reporter, I knew very little about poker and I'd never been to the US, let alone travelled on my own.

I was overwhelmed by the opportunity and unsure about

what to do: keep the secure career that looks great on paper, or jump into the terrifying unknown that feels so right?

One night I was at home, and the pressure was on to make a decision. I was crying and all worked up, not knowing what to do because I was so scared. I remember my mum sitting with me on my bed, calming me down. She told me to close my eyes and visualise two circles. One circle was staying in my current job, and the other circle was taking the new job. She had me visualise myself standing in one circle and seeing how I felt in there, and then standing in the other circle and seeing how that felt in comparison. She knew which one was making my heart sing, but she wanted to teach me how to listen to my own heart and make my decision for myself. It was that night that I decided to quit my job.

The next day I came home from work with a bottle of champagne. Mum opened the door and we started squealing in the doorway. Even though it meant seeing me leave for months at a time to travel thousands of miles away, she was, and still is, so incredibly supportive of me doing what makes my heart sing.

That was absolutely the best decision I have ever made for myself, and I have never looked back. I've been travelling the world for six years now, and I've manifested my childhood dream of living in Los Angeles and being on American prime-time television. That's all thanks to my mother's guidance.

With the beautifully balanced combination of make-up and self-empowerment, my mother has taught me to make sure I'm always being the best version of myself I can be, on the inside and out.

GRAEME SIMSION

Graeme Simsion traded life as a data modeller for
the creative pursuit of writing fiction – a move that
grabbed international attention with the success
of his debut novel, *The Rosie Project,* which has
sold more than a million copies in forty countries
around the world. His mother died when she
was 59 – the same age he was at the time of this
interview.

People ask if I have any regrets in my life and, always, the
first thing I say is: 'I didn't speak at my mother's funeral.'

I was 32 when my mother died, so she didn't have a chance
to meet my kids. She has been out of my life for a very long
time. I think it has had a bigger impact on our kids than on
me, in that my father remarried and then didn't have a lot
to do with our kids when they were quite young. I think he
connected much more with her grandchildren, as I think
happens when men remarry – they drift towards the family of
their new wife, instead of their own.

Pictured: June and Dennis Simsion with Graeme Simsion

I think, if my mother had lived and the world had gone as we had hoped – and she and my father had stayed together as you would expect – our kids would have had that additional connection with my side of the family. It's an impact that creates lots of ripples.

I think there was a lot of unfinished business with my mother, in the sense that I hadn't ever really let her know how much I appreciated what she did for me. I think I was probably pretty ungrateful and I hadn't communicated that. Mum had always been supportive. I was very busy getting on with my own life.

It was just one of those things that happen quite quickly. She had cancer but we didn't expect that she would die so suddenly. She was more ill than her doctors, or any of us, had realised and the funeral happened sooner than we had been preparing for.

I thought that my father would speak but he didn't and so we had the minister speak instead. He clearly did not know my mother well and it was, from my point of view, a bit shabby. I was really upset and angry, in retrospect, that she wasn't given a proper send-off.

I sat there thinking: 'I should really be up there to do this better.' The minister was doing all he could but it was like one of the introductions that you get when you speak at a conference or something – like someone has got the piece of paper in front of them and they are reading off it and there is no heart in it. I was sort of sitting there thinking, more than anything else, the solution would be my father's funeral, which I expect I should still be alive for – he turns 90 next year. It will be a very small funeral because his friends are gone and so that will be my chance, I think, to sort of talk to the family about how I feel about both of them.

One of my colleagues asked me, for God knows what reason: 'Do you have any regrets in your life?' She would have only been in her twenties at that time and I was probably in my late forties – and I told her about the funeral.

A few months later, her father died in a car accident. He was a well-known person – a well-connected person – and she got up at the funeral and did this fantastic speech, so, I thought, in a way, that my regret had been able to translate into something worthwhile.

Because my father remarried quite quickly – within twelve months – after my mother's death, the memories of my mother have been swept away a little. You get those two extremes where my father might have chosen to mourn for the rest of his life – he was in his sixties – and, you know, the house would have been a shrine and we would have felt awkward going in there. Or, the other extreme is what we had – he got on with a new life and she disappeared and all the memories were pulled out of our lives quite quickly.

It was difficult, so we lost not only concrete things but also emotional things you can't ever get back. I have some bits and pieces of her jewellery and that's about it. Because my wife only met my mother on a few occasions, she didn't really get to know her in any substantial way so we don't have that connection of shared memories either.

I have two siblings – both younger, both girls, both still living and making their own lives. My younger sister was still living at home when my mother died and she left home very shortly after that. I think she feels it most acutely that her mother wasn't around for her. I think for women particularly, when they have children and are in that very early stage, when they are looking for someone who can look after their children, the mother is the first port of call.

I think, with parents in general, everybody has got a different trajectory. There are some guys I know who have been very close to their mothers all the time – relationships where you see that bond between mother and son is not only very strong but also very open – and they say things like: 'I love my mother, she is the most important person in my life.'

I think that, for me and my mother, it was probably true that the bond was very strong but because I came from an Anglo-Saxon background, you didn't express that. Also, I think, in the Anglo-Saxon world, there is not this thing about mothers loving their sons more than their daughters. It was probably the other way around.

I grew up in New Zealand until I was twelve and then we moved to Australia. Our conventional middle-class family meant that my mother didn't go to work. Now it is the norm within the middle class that both parents have careers and work.

There was a whole nuclear family sort of model there that I very explicitly didn't want to follow. I think, even if society hadn't seen this massive switch towards women in the workforce, I would have still been interested in finding a partner who was engaged in other aspects of the world, rather than being a stay-at-home mother. I didn't want to marry 'her'.

I didn't see my mother and father having, for want of a better word, an intellectual relationship. My mother was a long way from being stupid – she was an intelligent woman who was a secretary of the town clerk in Auckland before she had kids. I am sure her IQ was similar to dad's IQ but both of them grew up in circumstances where boys were privileged and women didn't pursue their own careers.

In my own life, I didn't want to go home to someone who looked after the kids. I was interested in someone who was an equal in every sense and I expected that I would do my share and she would do hers. In that sense, my parents' relationship was in no way a role model for the one that I wanted. It wasn't problematic in a big way – it just wasn't what I was looking for.

I didn't appreciate that she was always there for us when we got home from school – it was just normal: I saw my dad's job as going out to work and hers as staying at home. I didn't sense that her job was more onerous than my father's but I certainly sensed that it was less respected.

When we moved from New Zealand to Australia it was because my father had an opportunity for a job over here. There was some consultation that went on but I think 'no' would have been the wrong answer from her. I felt very displaced but not as displaced as my mother. I think, in retrospect, my mother was probably clinically depressed when we came to Australia. She was close to her family, she had friends – she would have been in her late thirties when we moved to Australia, almost forty. So, it was a difficult time in life when you reassess and stuff and, of course, she didn't come here as my father did and immediately go into a job where you have all those sorts of supports waiting for you.

Dad was very busy with a big project and working long hours and Mum was so unhappy. In many ways, I think that created some separation between me and her, as I sort of forged my own path.

I was twelve, and it was very difficult for me because I was in a class with kids two years older than me. In those days, you went with the academic standing, rather than social standing, so I was socially very displaced – all of which was to prove useful to me later in life because I was able to write a book about a guy who was socially displaced. And even though I didn't have Asperger's syndrome, I had a sense of what it was like to not be one of the gang – to be bullied and all those sorts of things.

I was forging a pretty independent sort of life. Not independent physically, in the sense of leaving home, or even being particularly adventurous in travelling or anything by myself – but emotionally and intellectually, I was pretty self-contained.

The great thing I had from my mother was acceptance – during every age, and, I think, of all three of us. She had some very strong sorts of moral values but, given that I wasn't visibly stepping outside of those, she was just openly supportive.

My father had ambitions for me, which were not of that kind of 'my child will be a doctor' or 'my child will be a whatever' – it wasn't like that. It was more that he instilled a sense that a real man can do certain things – you've got to be able to do carpentry, you've got to be able to ride a bike – and I was, physically, a pretty awkward sort of kid.

My mum was never on my case – whatever I wanted to do, that was fine. You know, if I wanted to collect coins, or stay in my room, or whatever – it wasn't that she didn't care, it was just that she was accepting of who I was. Whereas, I think my father had a clearer idea in his mind about what a boy should be. I have to say, though, that was probably good for me to have those two influences in my life. If I only had my mother, I think I would have missed out on some things that were probably character-building, you know. And if I had only had my father, I would have probably felt that I couldn't develop those parts of me that didn't fit the mould.

I think that I am a pretty accepting person – my wife would say that is the example my mother set for me. Maybe it was that I needed acceptance and therefore I would naturally give it to others. I think it's interesting.

If you were bullied, then there are two likely outcomes. The first is that you understand what it is like to be bullied and therefore you make sure that others are not bullied as you get more power in your life. The second is that you choose to bully somebody else. I think you see that in schools – that, actually, some of the worst bullies have been bullied themselves and simply find someone further down the social hierarchy to set the mob on. I have probably touched on the second one a couple of times in my life, to my shame. But I have also become someone who is pretty accepting of other people and I think this has affected my parenting in a big way.

If you were to ask what my mother gave me, I think I'd say that, in the parenting of our children, my wife Anne and I have adopted a very similar model to what my parents did, but with our gender-roles reversed. I tend to be the 'whatever you want' parent. Anne went through a much stricter sort of upbringing in terms of being told: 'You need to be a doctor, you need to be something important.' I don't think I ever put those expectations on the kids. Anne would say I don't set them any boundaries but they would say that the boundaries were always there, in terms of subtle expectations of proper behaviour and so forth. Anne would be much clearer: 'You can't do this, but you can do that.'

My mother talked a lot about her origins, about her family and the family history, and I wasn't really interested but it was obviously important to her. The iconic story in her life was that her own mother died at the age of fifty-nine. So, it was a really big deal – my mother came of age at the same time her mother died. In her eyes, her mother was on an absolute pedestal.

When we grew up, she told us a lot about her mother and we didn't relate to it because she was dead and we were young, you know – it was not something we wanted to deal with, particularly. 'Your grandmother is in heaven,' she would say. We would be thinking: 'Don't bother telling us this – we don't need to know.'

She died of cancer and of course my mother had this thing about her mother dying at fifty-nine, and then my mother proceeded to do the same thing at fifty-nine.

Now, I realise that my mother had just wanted that legacy to go on – that's why the stories were important to her.

In New Zealand, all of my mother's siblings are now dead – three of them, including my mother, died within three months and the last one died quite a few years ago, at ninety. My sister who's two years younger than me stays much better connected to all the cousins through Facebook.

I am currently fifty-nine and Anne gave me a bit of a hard time about it. You worry about this, but not consciously. The women have not done well in my family. My father's mother died at thirty-five in childbirth, so it is not a good link all around, really.

I'm fortunately in pretty good shape but it does remind you that life is finite. I did a talk at the Brisbane Writers Festival – Letter To My Future Self – and I decided to address myself at eighty-nine, which is thirty years on, and my dad is eighty-nine now, so that was actually quite uplifting to think that there could be thirty more years for me. I could start playing the piano now and I have thirty years to learn to play. I still feel that, with a bit of luck, I will live a very long life and still have a lot of time to do things. My mother died too young.

So, what would I say to myself at eighty-nine? Well, I would finish by saying: 'I hope you learned how to play the bloody piano – you have had enough time to do it.'

I certainly feel that I have enough time to write the books that I want to write. It is nice to think that I would live long enough to have grandchildren and be known to them and have a role in their lives. Our kids are now in their twenties and this is all stuff on the horizon.

When I had my first book published, my father said: 'I never knew you had this bent.' He looked astonished. 'Why on earth would you write a book now?'

I confided a great deal in my mother when I was young. I didn't feel I had to hide things from her and I think she had a pretty good sense that I had those sorts of mixed talents. When I was at intermediate school in New Zealand, I was actually dux of the school and the headmaster called me in and said: 'You are an unusual person because you have strengths in both the scientific side and also in writing and, at some point in your life, I guess you are going to have to decide which path to follow.' But I just thought it was a ludicrous statement at the time – obviously, I was going to follow science.

But all through my career, I've written, I've spoken, I've

communicated and it has probably been the most important string to my bow, really. I am not a brilliant scientist but I am a very strong communicator.

I think I was twenty-two when I left home and, really, I was pursuing other things, so I would call my mum once a week or she would call me. I was very consciously separated from the family and building my own life and my mother had the ability to see through all of that. I think my partner sees through me and my kids see me pretty well. I don't have stuff to hide, particularly. What you see is what you get.

Obviously, when Mum died, my father was very upset. It didn't knock him off his perch – if anything, it made it easier for him to be the patriarch. He no longer had to care for my mother in the last few months of her life because she was becoming quite dependent and having medical problems.

Now as my father has aged and he is in a nursing home, I guess I am the senior member of the family – but it doesn't have the same meaning. My sisters are in their fifties too and have their own families and their own capabilities – I don't think there is a need for a family leader.

I have married twice and both times my partner has been a professional, educated, intelligent woman, making her own life and expecting me to pull my share of the weight in all things. I have been very happy about that arrangement.

I have a book that is in the editing stages at the moment and there are two important mother characters in there and my wife thinks I based both of them on her mother – you know, the dark side and the good side. There is always probably a little bit of truth in that – you are always inspired by people around you but I don't think I have written a mother character yet who has been driven much by my own mother. Possibly, I think with Don Tillman's mother in *The Rosie Project*, there is probably a bit of my mother in her but, you know, nothing that would jump straight out at you.

Had I known she was going to die so young, in the last years of her life I would have engaged more with her, and shown more interest in some of the things that she was interested in that I tended to brush off. I think that I could have probably spent more time with her.

There is one really strong memory of my mother, although it might be more about me than her, really. When my grandfather died, the funeral was on the fifth of November 1965, which was Guy Fawkes Day, and back in those days you used to do fireworks. My dad said: 'We are not going to do the fireworks,' and my mum came home and she said: 'We will do the fireworks.' I remember she was tremendously upset at the death of her father – she just held her parents in such an extremely high regard, and as a nine-year-old kid, I wasn't connected to how much that mattered. I just took the death of my grandfather pretty much in my stride. I mean, to me, he was an 86-year-old smoker who was coughing all the time and he was on the point of death anyway, in my mind. But for my mother, it was her Dad and she loved him so much – and now I look back and see that extraordinary emotion, and her sense to still be a good mother and let the kids have their fireworks, was something very significant. It was a very small incident, really, but it just popped into my mind.

In the sixties and early seventies, you didn't drink wine with meals at home, you didn't ever go out to restaurants – money mattered a lot and you reused things. I remember my mother bottling and preserving everything – nothing was wasted – and if there is anything that is a carryover from my mother, in particular, it's that I have this thing about using every bit of food we have. It translates to me in quite a perverse way, really. We might have chicken stock that I know will only last a few days, so I will go out and buy all the other ingredients to make the soup. Or, we'll have an avocado that's getting soft and so I will go out and make sure we have the rest of the ingredients to make a guacamole.

If I go to the fridge and there is mouldy food, it hits me in some way that we are being irresponsible. That is probably the most living legacy of my mother – that every day it hurts me in a fiscal way to waste food.

After dinner my mother would wash the dishes and I would dry the dishes and we would always have conversations. I told her all about the stuff I was interested in – about maths and physics and that sort of thing. I don't know what level of comprehension she had for that but she knew I was excited about it and interested and she gave me an audience. She never said: 'Oh look that's boring, Graeme,' or: 'Why do I want to know that?' She just listened to all of it and if I had tried that with anybody else, you know, I would have got 'shut up' or 'not interested' or 'why are you telling me this stuff?'

That was just my time with my mother – although I bet my sisters would say that they dried the dishes too, and it may well be true, but my memories are only of the nights when it was me doing them. It was my time with my mother and something that was always there. I felt that it was fantastic.

We have a deal with our kids now that, once a week, we have to have dinner around the table together. They are adults, still living at home, and they are both still students. One of the deals about being allowed to live at home with free rent is that we have dinner and you can bring your partners and we sit around this table. In that way, we are preserving a little bit of that connection – having those conversations. It is important.

JACQUELINE PASCARL

Many Australians remember her as Jacqueline
Gillespie – the former television newsreader
and radio host, who was caught in a dramatic
international battle for her children, when they
were taken, seven years after the couple's divorce, to
live with their father. Jacqueline eventually reunited
with her adult children and is now an author,
columnist, National Vice Chair of the Australian
Defence Reserves and sits on many medical and
charitable boards.

I f you ask me what I learned from my mother, it's that it is
possible for a person to be a biological parent yet relinquish
all affection and all care. I really had an absence of both mother
and father growing up.

My mother was mentally unstable, probably from the time
I was born, if not earlier. Compounding that, when I was two,
my mother had a cerebral embolism from using prescribed
medication and she was clinically dead for eight minutes. It

Pictured: Jacqueline Pascarl with her godmother Constance Coverdale left her with temporal lobe epilepsy and scarring on her brain, so that just compounded the mental illness.

My mother was more of a shadowy figure in the background of my childhood. She was there but she wasn't mothering. I divided my time between my godmother and my grandmother. My godmother, especially, was the closest thing I had to a traditional mum.

My godmother and my godfather – Auntie Connie and Uncle Kevin – are amazing, salt of the earth, fantastic people who didn't have any other children until I was eight. We lived an amazing life up on a dairy farm in Gippsland. I got all my good sense and my warped sense of humour and unflappability from my godmother.

I was living with my grandmother during school time and my godmother during holiday time. There was no school near her up in the country because they were miles out of town.

Day one of prep, I knew I was different.

I went to an Anglo-Catholic school in the south-eastern suburbs of Melbourne and I looked like the Vietcong. I was half-Chinese, and my grandmother was titian-haired with green eyes – a diminutive Jewish lady. She would nurture me with music and dance and cultural things. She was a milliner and she loved fabrics and so we sewed and we did some embroidery together.

In prep I got an idea that I was different when the other children were being moved away from the coloured girl, which was me, apparently. The parents had complained. I had mud and sticks and stones and plums and gravel from the street thrown at me. They were singing *ching, chong, ning, nong* all the way home.

I was four years old – how should a child process that?

I had a couple of friends, sporadically, thoughout primary school, but I read and I read and I wrote and I wrote. I read and I wrote. I wrote and I read. That was it.

I went to two birthday parties in the entirety of my primary school life. One was for a girl with a harelip and I was very grateful – she was lovely. But the other one who invited me, the entire party was tormenting me – it made the movie *Mean Girls* look like amateur hour.

What made it worse was that I was a gun at English and great at social studies. I was quite clever, so I got the double whammy. I've got slanty eyes and I'm being brought up with no reference to Asia at all, you know. I was watching Fred Astaire and Ginger Rogers movies and, ironically, all of my grandmother's family fought on the Kokoda Trail.

Because of both my godparents and my grandmother, I had a very Anglo background. It was just my packaging that was different. Australia wasn't this multicultural society back then. The only new Australians, really, were Italians and Greeks and Maltese, mainly. There was no intermarriage between Australians and Asians. My parents were spat at on the street when my mother was pregnant with me – and my father was a highly educated university graduate.

In the olden days, as I tell my kids, godparents were meant to have been chosen to step into the breach, should anything happen to the biological parents.

Auntie Connie and Uncle Kevin were incredible. They said: 'They just don't understand – your name is Jacqueline and that's it. This is your home, everything is fine. People terrorise those who are different out of ignorance.'

My mum wasn't around much during those early years, but then she came back into my life and I went to live with her. She had been an in-patient at a psychiatric hospital and came out with a man she'd met across a crowded group therapy session, and they both sexually abused me from the age of ten.

I didn't tell my godmother because I knew that if I told anyone and Mum found out, I'd be stopped from seeing Auntie Connie. I'd already been cut off from my grandmother very abruptly when my mother took custody of me.

I danced ballet. That was it for me – and books. I withdrew to survive. My grandmother had introduced me to dance. For me, it was the perfect form of escape.

My mother had several nervous breakdowns while I was living with her. I became her primary carer and she isolated herself – her relationship broke up temporarily. I did all the banking, I did all the washing, I had to learn to cook. I had to take her to the doctor and I'd medicate her too. She fell in a heap when the boyfriend walked out for a while. I had to become an adult at ten years old. Their relationship was on and off for a year and then my mother's boyfriend came back into our lives and the abuse began again.

They threatened that if I told anyone what was going on, they would withdraw ballet, so I kept quiet. I stopped writing and I just toed the line to survive, waiting for the time when I would be legally allowed to leave home and earn a living. I read all the time. Music and literature are ways of connecting with humanity and learning – knowledge is power.

You realise that one has to work at being a good human being and that's what I decided I would do – and work at being a good parent when I became a mum. I wanted to create a functional, working family where I would be a parent and I would love a child unconditionally – I suppose that's the phrase, isn't it? I don't think we love anyone unconditionally. I think we love with a depth and breadth of commitment. I know I felt that all through my parenting years. It sounds such a terrible wank to say this but I really truly believe that when you have a child and you look into that baby's eyes for the first time, you create a covenant with that child that's unbreakable. You have a duty to remain steadfast and love deeply and support and nurture – and distance and time and separation don't negate that covenant.

I understand that, possibly, my mother had postnatal depression, compounded by mental illness and ill health – and the 'mother's little helpers' that the doctors were prescribing in the sixties. But I don't think anything excuses abuse of a child. I don't think that past life experiences negate the moral commitment you have to have towards a child.

There's a point in everyone's life where you just make a decision: 'Am I going to inflict the same treatment on someone else, or am I going to move forward and change what is supposedly my statistical destiny?'

You have to take responsibility for your life.

I made a conscious decision to talk to my children as though they weren't idiots because my godmother always spoke to me like I was an intelligent, but smaller person.

She is a natural educator. She's a great gesticulator with her hands and she lights up any room when she talks. She has a wry sense of humour, so I learned dry humour from her and I learned to parent from her and if ever I needed a role model to think about how I would tackle a situation, I would say: 'What would my Auntie Connie say?'

She never tried to formally adopt me and become my mother legally. Connie is correct in everything that she does. She is very respectful of other people's boundaries and she would never presume to put words in anyone's mouth.

I have always muttered under my breath: 'Hey, Auntie Connie – Mum', 'Uncle Kevin – Dad'. Always.

My mother subjugated my needs for her wants and her desires and I am very bitter about it. I make no bones about it. But I took a deep breath and moved on – it's not something I revisit every day. I went to therapy in my late twenties after my own children were kidnapped and I dealt with a lot of stuff. I don't use her name publicly – she is entitled to her privacy. I am entitled to mine, in that respect, too. It just doesn't need airing. I don't need my day in court. She will never have anything to do with my children. She never has and she never will. I think of both her and my step-father as an infection.

I just accepted it – that that was the way my life was. I had different compartments and one was utterly full of soft cushions and farm life and that was my godmother. The other was my mother.

Both my godparents are phenomenal. It was never a sexist relationship between them. She does the cooking because she is better at it but they have such an equal relationship that it is quite inspiring – and well before women's lib. It was my touchstone of how things should be.

I was seventeen years old when I married first. I didn't have enough intellectual maturity to look at the onion-like layers of a relationship. I didn't understand that beyond the romance you should be looking for parity on all levels.

I think my godmother sat back and just let me. I was a

bit of a steam engine. She is not one to lay down the law. I wish now, with the maturity I have now, that people would have said to me: 'Hey, this is not such a great idea.' But, you know, marrying at seventeen – I wasn't listening to anyone. I was in love with the idea of being in love and I wasn't seeing my godmother very often by then anyway because I had developed a life in the city.

It is wonderful, the relationship that we have now. I feel that I can still go up and ask for a cuddle – even at my age and with her in her eighties. We have a woman-to-woman relationship now, which is quite a revelation, but then I see her dealing with my children and she is back to the sort of mothering she gave me.

I think the relationship I have with Auntie Connie is similar on many levels to mother-daughter relationships that I see amongst my friends – but there are also gaps, I think, possibly, because she felt that she could never fully, legally lay down the law to me or guide me or forbid me to do certain things, other than when I was little. There is also the tyranny of distance – she lives a two- or three-hour drive from where I live. Still, I know I can pick up the phone and just discuss everything with her. She is a good conversationalist. I can spend a couple of hours on the phone, backwards and forwards, asking for advice and talking to her about things.

She was amazing during the years of the kidnap. She was someone I could go to and cry with, or just sit with. She's whip-smart, so she would follow all of the nuances of things – both from what she was told by me and what was coming out of the press.

It has been very important to me that my children view

both Auntie Connie and Uncle Kevin as the closest thing that they have got to grandparents.

They only see her infrequently but when she sees them, she's interested. She's always present. I've seen a lot of other people grandparent and they ask the standard: 'How's school? Got any friends? That's nice, would you like something to eat?'

She talks to them, she engages, she remembers facts, she remembers the names of their friends, she knows their scholastic shining moments and the things that they need help in. She's like a Rolodex of their likes, dislikes – and their foibles.

She has never – throughout my entire life – forgotten me on my birthday or Christmas. She is a great card and letter writer. She would always write to me once a week and she is still trying to do that with my children.

She is strict. She loves to say: 'Eat those vegetables.' She will give a smaller portion to my youngest but she expects him to eat. She is big on feeding kids up and feeding me up. She still considers me too slim – even today – but she considered me positively emaciated when I was 47 kilograms in the middle of a crisis. She's the sort of person who will always call a spade a spade.

I bake – she taught me that. She's a sterling baker. A Country Women's Association amazing baker – all the recipes are in her head, more or less. Pastry, shortbreads, plum puddings, Christmas cakes – everything. Her Christmas cakes are legendary. The most confronting thing she has recently said to me is: 'No, I am not baking them any more – I am just buying Lions Club ones, so here's the recipe.'

For years, I tried to get the family shortbread, plum pudding and Christmas cake recipes from her and she wouldn't hand them over. She would sometimes give one to me but I suspect one of the ingredients was always left out. It was never right. But she recently sat me down and dictated all the family recipes to me as I wrote them out on my laptop – all the family recipes. Really, I wanted to weep. I wanted the recipes all my life but now that I've got them, I don't want them any more. It's what it represents. She has an underlying medical condition, which means that I could speak to her on the phone today or she could sit in her chair this afternoon and not be with us tomorrow. She knows she is living with a ticking time bomb and yet she continues to bake and make jams and chutneys – I forgot to mention them before, fabulous jams and chutneys – plus she's captain of her croquet team.

Every winter they drive to Alice Springs to see their other daughter, Judith, who is a teacher up there, so Auntie Connie spends a couple of months a year with her. She gardens every day and she grows her own vegetables and I have adopted that habit now too. I'm growing things and they are giving me seeds and instructions.

I feel like I can never thank her enough. She made me the resilient person I am now and gave me the foundation that made me able to turn into a decent person – and to parent properly – and able to grow into someone she is proud of.

I should really be shooting up in a corner, self-harming, abusing my children, selling my kids on the street for sex or be long since dead. I could have been one of those people and the only reason I am not is because of her.

As of next week, my eldest daughter, Shah, will be living here full-time. She is moving back to Australia with her husband and her little daughter – and I've got a new grandchild on the way. After everything we went through, we are really close now. Really close. She insisted that I call her and be on the phone for twenty-seven hours during her first labour, so, even though I was still in Melbourne, I was present in the room with her too.

She asks me all sorts of nuts and bolts parenting questions, although I do worry that Google has replaced the grandparents – Grandma Google.

I breastfed Shah for twenty months and I think she has breastfed her own child for that long, if not longer. She was not with me from when she was seven years old and two days, until she was twenty-and-a-half years old.

So she was gone fourteen years with no contact.

When she was growing up it was torturous for me knowing that she was going through puberty without me and her teenage years of revolt without me – without me as a point of reference to vilify and castigate and learn from and love.

We have both reconciled to the fact that we can't claw those years back and now we talk all the time. We have two- or three-hour conversations on Skype and I could be doing something in the kitchen and shooting the breeze while she is doing something else at the other end.

We just talk as if we are in the same room together, with parallel activities, and she has made that a big part of my granddaughter's life. I am called 'Gug' – not Grandma or Grandmamma or Nanna. It just evolved and I really like the concept of having your own unique grandmotherly name.

I mustn't underplay the role my own nanna played in my

life – in raising me. She was incredible but she was so much older than me. She died in her nineties and I was twenty-eight – she was a very elderly grandmother. She didn't have her own child until she was in her forties.

I never saw her without clothes on. Ever. She had this voluminous flannelette nightie that she used to put on. When I was living with her, during all the school terms, we were in single beds, separated by a dressing table. She would put hair rollers in at night, she would say her rosary, she even had a chamber pot underneath her bed because the loo was outside. She was a classic Scarlett O'Hara – she would sew my clothes from curtains that she found in the op shop or remnants of clothes that she would pick apart and resew into fabric. I had the worst clothes growing up – they were just utterly inappropriate for my age. I wore different clothes on the farm than I did down in town but my grandmother was always immaculately presented – she'd have a hat, gloves and high heels. Her shoes all had a heel on them.

One thing I always remember about her is that every night the light would go off in the bedroom we shared, and then you would hear 'clink' and she would be taking her dentures out and putting them in a glass beside the bed.

I am quite a strict parent. As parents we are there to raise them, to teach them, to nurture them, to be their sounding board and also be there to help with the heartbreak when they are going to make a bad decision.

Friendship with our children, as I have learned, comes later. You are not your children's friend until they are an adult, and you shouldn't be. I really feel quite nauseous when I see the magazine articles where women in their mid- to late-thirties are saying: 'My eight-year-old daughter is my best friend we have manicures together.' My message to women like that is this: You have got a problem if you think that your seven-year-old is your friend – you really need to get out more because that is just not the way that life is meant to be.

I had ovarian cancer and I was told in no uncertain terms by the cancer specialists – this was in September – that I would be lucky to make it to December.

Shah came home, and my son Iddin, so all four kids were together and the eldest two were absolutely horrified. All they could say was: 'No, the little ones need you – they *need* you.' They were emphatic.

They missed me and needed me when they were growing up and I wasn't there, through no fault of ours, but because outside forces separated us. I knew that they needed me. Now, here were my older children who had been separated from me for fourteen years throughout their formative teenage years, begging me to fight and to stay alive. It was as though they were caught in some sort of cyclone and they were screaming at me from a distance: 'You have to stay because Verity and Zane need you – you cannot die, you cannot die.'

It was devastating because we had talked about it in intellectual terms. There had been tears and all those sorts of things but when faced with losing me again, their thoughts were for themselves, yes, but they were primarily for their younger siblings – that no one else in our family should have to do without me, that mum is so important. I can't comment from personal experience because I had a very strange childhood, but I know that my children who were without me for all those years didn't want their younger brother and sister to be without me as they had been.

My hands, I hate them. I don't like to look down at my hands because they are so similar to hers, and those hands did terrible things to me. I know I don't have her body, her voice – she was blonde with blue eyes, so I don't look like her.

Nature versus nurture? Nurture for me. And it is not me just rejecting my mother because of the tough time I had with the abuse, it's that I made a decision to adopt the characteristics of my godmother and I made a decision to adopt the best parts of my grandmother – and the rest I made up myself.

ADRIANO ZUMBO

The Australian pâtissier came to our national
attention on *MasterChef* when his complex
desserts were dished up as challenges to the show's
contestants. Adriano Zumbo grew up in country
New South Wales as the son of Italian immigrants
and had simple beginnings, baking packet cake
mixes at the local supermarket bakery his family
owned. His perception of his mother is as a
proud woman who worked hard for her success.
Her sacrifices continue to inspire his own work
ethic, but remind him to take the time to enjoy
life as well.

I pretty much grew up living in a supermarket. My parents
owned a local supermarket in a small country town now
called Coonamble in central New South Wales. It had just
3,000 people – very small.

I think it was because I spent so much time in the supermarket, but I was more into the sweet smells – those artificial

Pictured: Adriano Zumbo and Nancy Zumbo

smells. I loved it. The supermarket was full of lollies and I could take them for free. I used to fill my school bag with all the junk food I could.

It definitely had a big influence on who I am now. It's given me a great understanding of what's out there and at the moment, in the dessert world, you can see people get their inspiration from so many things that go back to childhood. Everything is about nostalgia.

Really, I love to create crazy things – crazy flavours off the cuff – but not a lot of people want all that stuff, so if you want to appeal to the masses, you give them flavours that they know and the things they're familiar with. If you make something with black olives and yoghurt and green apples, you know, you may get people who would want to try it but if they saw it on a menu next to something else made with Snickers – something they recognise – they'll probably choose that. There's always some people who are daring but the majority of people go for the norm.

I get that. My childhood was completely Italian. Our backyard was all chickens, veggie garden, fruit trees everywhere. And I just wanted to be the average Aussie kid. Mum always cooked Italian food but I didn't appreciate it at all. I was a very fussy eater. She would sit there with the wooden spoon and she would just hit the table until I ate it – she did not give up. Sometimes she would sit there for hours trying to get me to eat things I didn't want. Even the Italian desserts – custards and all kinds of great things. I didn't want any of it. (I still don't like cream. I don't mind if it's mixed in other things but I don't like the texture.) Now I realise the stuff Mum was feeding me was all amazing food – beautiful food – but it was the smells, as a kid, I didn't like. And I would be really rude about it too. I would say: 'I'm not eating that – it stinks.'

I used to talk to my mum while she was cooking but I didn't hang around as much as I should have. I was into sports and I was out with my mates constantly – I was never home.

It was a definitely a love-hate thing between my mum and me when I was a teenager. Around fourteen or fifteen – I was not the perfect son. I was always sneaking out and climbing down the balcony and the guys would pick me up around nine o'clock, when my folks thought I was in bed. I'd climb out the balcony and my mates would hold their hands out and I'd step out on their hands, then onto the fence – and then I'd go out all night.

Mum never knew, until the baker told her she saw me buying a sausage roll around three o'clock in the morning and Mum was like: 'What?'

That's when it all came out and she was not impressed. She started threatening me that she'd got a sensor light and an alarm to tell when I was coming out of my room, but a couple weeks later I did it again so it was never actually true about the alarms and everything. It was always a threat – just her trying to scare me.

I have two sisters. One is twelve years older and one's ten years older than me. Around that time, they built one of my sisters a supermarket on the other side of town to have an extra business and it had its own bakery. She was twenty-something and she'd been living in Sydney, but then she came back to Coonamble when my parents bought the business for her. I started working in that shop, rather than my parents' shop, just because it was newer and more fun. I started making cakes, frying donuts – simple stuff. It wasn't rocket science, you know. I was using packet cake mixes to do the cakes – maybe adding things to make them a bit different, or icing them a special way – it was very basic.

I wasn't doing very well at school. I was just interested in hands-on things, like metal work, woodwork, PE. I was good at geography, only because we used to play a game called *Where in the World is Carmen San Diego?* I used to play that in computer studies the whole time – I knew where all the countries in the world were. I also travelled a bit with my parents when I was young – we used to go to Italy every couple of years – so I got a B in geography. That was pretty much my best mark. I wasn't made for the academic world. By the time I finished my school certificate I had a job lined up in Sydney as an apprentice pastry chef.

I was fifteen when I left home and moved to Sydney. I moved in with my other sister. Mum was a bit shocked and a bit upset I wasn't going to take over the shop, which they wanted me to, but that's the way it was.

I never wanted to take over the business. I didn't have a great passion for it and I didn't want to sit behind a counter my whole life. In a way, it was easy money if I wanted to do it – easier than the apprenticeship, for sure – but I found the apprenticeship more enjoyable. I don't think I knew for sure that it was what I wanted to do for my whole life. In a way, it was a bit more of an escape. I was at that age where I just wanted to get away – getting an apprenticeship was an easy way of getting away from everything. I'd always enjoyed making cakes in my sister's shop before I left, but I didn't think I wanted to do it for a career. It was a bit of a gamble, really, but six months into the apprenticeship I knew I was doing something that I really enjoyed. I haven't looked back.

My sister said she'd put up with me staying with her. When I found the job in the paper she said: 'As long as it's okay with Mum and Dad, it's okay with me.' She used to drive me to work at 3 a.m. and then I'd catch the bus back home. She took on a big responsibility looking after me.

Because I hadn't been the best student or the best son, my mum and I had been fighting quite a bit, so it was good timing to get away from her and dad for a while.

My relationship with my mum is much better now. I mean, I don't see her enough because I'm in Sydney half the week – and half the week in Melbourne with my business there too – and she is still in Coonamble, but we do get along better. It was all me. It was nothing to do with her. Probably, it was just me at that age being a little shit and always causing trouble – always out with my mates, you know. Mum had this image, as all Italian parents do, that the son is meant to take over and work in the business and they want you to be this person, but I wasn't being that person. I wasn't going to do what they wanted me to do, you know. They weren't in control.

Even after years of me being away, when I was a few years into my apprenticeship, they had exactly the same hope – every year they would ask me when I was coming back. Every year I had to tell them that I didn't want to give up my apprenticeship and I didn't want to come back. It was an argument that went on for a few years.

Coonamble is about a seven-and-a-half hour drive from Sydney. For the first year, I used to go home every weekend because I still played footy in Coonamble. I'd drive up Saturday, play footy on Sunday, then drive back to Sydney ready for work Monday morning. I stopped playing for the football team after a year and after that, I visited less and less – maybe I'd go home for Easter and a few other times during the year, and eventually I pretty much just went home for Christmas.

Mum's definitely said she's proud of me and especially since I've been on *MasterChef*, because that's a way for her to be able to see what I do – and to see the way other people react to what I do. My parents watch the show and say: 'That's my son, that's my son!' I think for the first four or five years, there was a lot of doubt about what I was doing and they'd say: 'What do you want to be a baker for?' But over the years, I think I've sort of changed their attitude. Now my mum even drops my name when she goes to restaurants, to try and get a table if it's busy. She told me. She'll say: 'I am Adriano Zumbo's mother.' I am so glad I'm not there.

That's the type of woman she is – she'll try and use anything if it helps her get something. She's a bargainer. Sometimes, you know, people might misjudge her, because she's a bit of a nagger and can be sort of angry. She is a beautiful woman, and a great mum – very caring, very loving, and would do anything for you.

I do remember her being angry when I was a child. I didn't understand it then. I think maybe she was frustrated. She worked very hard and she didn't have control over a lot of things in her life. I think the only thing she would have really loved to do is garden. I think that's the only career she would have ever wanted to chase. When she wasn't working, she was always in the garden.

Mum never wanted to go back to Italy – actually, she hated

Italy. There were a few problems back there with her family. In the early days, when I was really young, my grandmother came out and lived with us for a bit in Coonamble and back then I think it was all good. But back in Calabria, there was fighting between the other sisters – fighting about money and property. Dad came out to Coonamble because his brother was already there and so my parents opened a supermarket and had a bit more of a life, whereas in Italy, especially in southern Italy, it's a little bit more villagey. For my mum, Australia was better – but I think that was because of her family.

My dad loves Italy still and he spends three months a year hanging with his other brothers and sisters. He goes over during the summertime and always has a great time. Mum? I think she's been maybe once in ten or fifteen years.

I was speaking Italian until I was four. My parents do speak dialect to me now and then, but because I went to school in a country town with no other multicultural influence – just Australians and Indigenous Australian people – I didn't want to speak it in front of my friends back then. My parents used to speak Italian to me but I'd say: 'What are you talking about?' My friends would be looking at my folks like they didn't have a clue what was going on. I just wanted to fit in with everybody else. I didn't want to be different.

When I was a kid, I ate pasta with no sauce, ham sandwiches, roast potatoes, steak – but it had to be a certain thickness and it had to be overcooked – hot chips, and the rest was junk food.

Since I became a chef I've learned to appreciate Mum's cooking – I eat everything. Now she can cook whatever she wants for me. I look forward to seeing her to see what she's going to cook – I love her ravioli. After all the challenges we had when I was a teenager and how hard a time I gave her when I was a kid, now the food has become our connection.

She's always told me what to do – that hasn't changed. She's a big watcher of TV cooking shows and then she always tries to give me tips she learns from the other shows. Oh my God – yeah, thanks Mum. She'll say something like: 'Did you know you've got to add this?' or 'You should add that'. Half the time I don't really listen but I just say: 'Oh, thanks.'

I make fun of it, but my parents have helped me heaps. I wouldn't have been able to open the business without them. Watching Mum and the way she worked so hard all my life, I learned that you've got to be strong. You don't get anything from sitting at home and not giving it a go. Get the right people around you and just keep going, and don't give up – doesn't matter what happens. Also, you've got to keep a look out for opportunity when it arises – I watched my parents do that.

My parents had no education. Back in Italy, my mum didn't go to school – I think she was there for just two years because her family couldn't afford to put her all the way through. It's quite an inspiration how successful my parents were with no education. It's the same with me – although I had a bit more education than they did – and what I've learned is that you don't have to be traditionally academically smart to be successful, and I think that's something that I cherish. It's a value that I try to give to my workers, and it's important because a lot of people who work for me are in the same boat – the way I was. Sometimes, they think they are nothing and sometimes I have to give out a more positive message. Just because you don't know nouns and verbs, it doesn't mean you're not smart.

There are different people out there – some people love academic knowledge and some people love to do things hands-on. Some people have a mind for putting things together and after being shown once they can go and do it themselves.

I don't remember this myself but my parents always told us this story: When my mum first came here and was in the supermarket, people from the town would come up to her and ask where the spuds were. But she didn't know what spuds were. She had tried so hard to learn all the English she thought she needed, including 'potatoes'. She had a really hard time trying to get used to everything. She really struggled and was often teased, I think. It affected her. Mum always had moments when she would just go off. Not so much at me, but just because she was having a hard time.

She's a tough woman, you know. She was by herself. She was isolated. I never knew her to have many friends back then. I mean, people knew her – they knew her and my dad because they ran the local supermarket. But they really only knew people because that's where everyone did their shopping. They weren't real friends.

They used to go straight to work six in the morning, then come home at eight at night. Most days I had to work a bit after school, maybe a couple of hours. Some days, I'd go to footy training and I would go home by myself – I pretty much always end up at home by myself.

When I went around to my friends' houses I'd see a huge difference. I noticed their parents were more involved in their lives. They used to go and watch them play footy, take them here, pick them up there, and they'd go on holidays together every few weeks somewhere – just camping or away for the night somewhere. I think I was a bit disconnected from my parents because they worked so hard.

When you come from nothing and you start to build something to survive, I think that once you start doing it, you just want to keep on doing it. I think their drive was trying to set up their kids with a great start. They put my sisters through boarding school but I didn't want to do that – I just wanted to stay at the school in town with my friends. When I was a kid, I found it scary being by myself in the house so much. But as I got older it shifted more into a sense of independence, and that's why moving out – leaving Mum and Dad – when I was fifteen wasn't that big a deal.

I didn't like being by myself so much while Mum was at work. It was hard when I was younger because I lived in this big house – one of those two-storey Italian houses with double columns. We had three rooms where no one ever set foot, with all the furniture covered in plastic to keep it perfect. There was a room with the telephone and a little table and plastic-covered chairs, and if I went in there to talk to my friends on the phone, Mum would come running in, yelling: 'Get your shoes off the furniture!' The whole plastic on the couch thing? Very Italian. It was just for show – these perfect unused rooms were all just for show.

Mum is not like that in other ways, but when it comes to jewellery, you see another side to my mum. She loves wearing diamond jewellery, gold jewellery – I think it's her way of showing how proud she is that she has been successful. She never had anything like that when she was growing up in

Calabria. Even at the supermarket her fingers would be covered in rings. She always liked looking nice and so she wore nice clothes and make-up.

It's why I named the high tea salon after her. I've got Little Frankie's after my dad and inside that, at the back, there's the tea salon which I named Fancy Nance. She loves that I've called it that.

I was the only kid from my group of friends who had to work – they'd always be asking me to come over or go here or there but I always had to work first, just for a couple of hours. My mum was a tough boss. I'm not as tough with my staff as she was with hers. She has the mentality that if her staff can't do the job properly, then she'll do it herself. I'm not like that. I think times have changed. Today, it's all about proper training and really getting your staff to believe in the culture of what you've tried to create in your business – making a happy place where people want to be part of your team. It was a little different back then, but it taught me how to be good with money.

Mum and Dad were very entrepreneurial. At one stage, they bought an old service station and Mum turned it into a chicken shop. It was her project. She did all this with no proper education – she just learned how to run a business by doing it. Then Dad had another business and opened a bottle shop. They always thought ahead and I really admire that. I was proud of her, the way she ran that chicken shop – she just recently sold it – and it's part of what has made me realise that I like to get my hands in a few different things too. I don't have just one aspect to my business.

That's why I've now got some of my products in super-markets, such as truffle mixes and cake mixes. Some people in my industry are very against it – they're purists but, I mean, just because I am a pastry chef, why can't I sell things in supermarkets? People think you're selling yourself out. Really, it's just a different option for a different market. People in the middle of a country town somewhere can't go to one of my stores and sit down and have a coffee and one of my desserts, but now they can go to the supermarket and try to do it at home.

As a child, I loved those cake mixes and pancake mixes – that's how I started in the bakery of my sister's shop, making those things and doing it my own way. I would take them to school and my teachers used to say: 'Wow, this is amazing! You should keep doing this.' It always made me feel good. Not much else used to make me feel good at school because I was always in trouble. I owe a lot to supermarket cake mix.

Mum loves the city and she used to come down to Sydney a lot, but she is definitely more of a country girl. She loves her garden, working in the shop, working in the community. Now everyone in Coonamble knows my mum and dad.

Mum is a big talker. She comes to visit me at my work sometimes and I have to keep her out of the kitchen – she starts talking to everybody and nobody gets any work done.

She hasn't talked about the fact that I'm not married for a while, but she used to – a lot. She'd say: 'Let's go back to Italy and I'll find you a beautiful girl.' I just say: 'That's all right, I'm sure I can find one here – I'll find her when the time is right.' But Mum always thinks she knows best.

KATHY LETTE

Her adolescence on Sydney's southern beaches in the 1970s was captured in *Puberty Blues* – the book the teenage Kathy Lette co-authored with a friend. With a string of other popular books behind her, the author and columnist now lives an expat life in London with her husband, Geoffrey Robertson. Kathy's relationship with her mother has always been a strong one. When Kathy's son was diagnosed with autism as a toddler, she says it was her mum who saved her sanity.

My mother gave me the greatest gift imaginable – three sensational sisters. We are great mates and love each other unconditionally. Well, there are a few conditions. Everyone must take their turn with the washing up, wine pouring and gin buying. But the only thing we really mock fight over is who is at the top of Mum's speed dial! We had the usual teen nightmares, when the generation gap seemed wider than the Simpson Desert, but through all our ordeals, Mum maintained

Pictured: Val Lette and Kathy Lette

her love and warmth. She's witty, wise, and wonderful. It must sound as though where there's a will, I really want to be in it! But I'm not being sycophantic or sentimental. Just ask any of my friends – they've all asked Mum to adopt them. Especially Ruby Wax, who wants to draw up legal papers.

My mum, Val, was a teacher. It was her absolute vocation, just like her mother before her. She was principal of infants and primary schools for as long as I can remember, and was absolutely adored by kids and parents alike. People still contact me all the time on Facebook and Twitter to tell me what a great teacher she was. She has that ability, that gift really, to see the potential in all her little charges, no matter how snot-faced, ankle-biting or just plain annoying.

My earliest memories of Mum are cupcakes and fairy stories and endless fun. It was a happy and carefree childhood. The most dangerous thing in a ten-mile radius was a bad oyster (the family home is on Oyster Bay). The lack of misery and hardship does not make a great childhood for a writer though – I've long contemplated suing my parents for loss of book royalties for bringing me up *too* happily. How could they be so friggin' inconsiderate?

My mother was always ahead of her time. She went to St George, a selective school for clever girls, just as her mother did before her. She was at teachers' college by seventeen. When she started teaching, she received six pounds a week. She gave two pounds to her mother, banked two for an overseas trip and lived on the rest. By twenty-one she was bound for Britain by boat, with a hat box and a gaggle of girlfriends, with whom she still meets once a month in town. All five of them lived in a tiny bedsit in Earls Court, boiling their eggs on the gas ring and hot-bedding. When they weren't teaching, they hitchhiked around Europe – long before it was fashionable.

She was a brilliant role model in that she inspired her four daughters to stand on our stilettoes and not ever wait to be rescued by a knight in shining Armani. That may sound pat, but it's a mantra of mine now and a lesson I always pass on to high school girls when I'm giving talks.

All through infants and primary school, I seem to remember that I had the only mum who worked. I was born in 1958, and the sixties was that era of lobotomised domesticity. It's captured so accurately by Betty Draper in *Mad Men*. Women were supposed to be decorative and demure – a life-support system to a womb. Having a mother who not only worked, but was also in a position of authority and power, ingrained into me the idea that women could do anything.

The Aussie men I grew up with disproved the theory of evolution – they were devolving into apes. In the Sydney suburbs in that era, 'Germaine Greer' was simply rhyming slang for beer. Mum says that when she read *The Female Eunuch* she was riveted – the book voiced so many of her secret thoughts and ideas. Germaine was like a front row forward feminist – a ball-kicker who cleared the field for the rest of us. Mum says she spent months defending Germaine at every suburban dinner party or barbecue. People would start badmouthing her and Mum would reply: 'Have you even read the book?' Of course they hadn't, so she would give a persuasive précis and slowly convert all the neighbourhood wives. My mum did go on to become Toastmistress champion of Australia, by the way, so she has a powerful way with words and a velvet-voiced delivery, which is magnetic and convincing. But feminism only went so far. She was supposed to represent Australia in the International Toastmistress championships in America, but with a full-time job and four kids, that was an impossibility.

I can remember winning writing competitions from the age of eight. My darling dad, Merv, was high up in the Post Master General's Department (PMG) at the time. They organised lots of painting and writing competitions across the state, and I seem to remember often winning the writing awards. I found all the rosettes and ribbons recently, hidden under the lining of Mum's linen press, which I found deeply touching, as we're not a sentimental family. Although we are loving and very huggy, we don't go in for a lot of big-noting. Affectionate teasing is our emotional modus operandi. 'Not a half-bad effort' is the equivalent of a Shakespearean love sonnet. And 'good on you' is like winning the Nobel Prize.

Because Mum was a teacher, she was obviously devastated when I dropped out of school at sixteen. Really traumatised! I always say that the only examination I've ever passed is my cervical smear test, but I was actually a straight-A student. Well, apart from maths. I am totally innumerate. (I cling to the old joke – how does it go? Why are Aussie women so bad at maths? Because men are always telling them that six inches equals ten.) I so wanted to be a writer and couldn't wait to get out into the world to find things to write about. I couldn't understand why teachers spent all those years teaching you to talk, then just made you shut up. I do regret it now, though. I'm an autodidact – which is clearly a word I taught myself.

Getting an honorary doctorate from Southampton Solent

University a few years ago was the highlight of my life – and my mum's. She was even more thrilled than I was. When the University rang me to ask for my head size for the doctoral cap, I remember saying: 'Well it was much smaller before you asked me that question!' I wore that bloody cap everywhere – to the shops, to the gym. I even wore it in the shower, covered in a shower cap! Leaving school prematurely was a great incentive to succeed – just to prove to my academic mum that I could make it some other way.

What my mum and I do share is a love of words. We are cruciverbalists and do the Guardian crossword every day by Skype. And we get it out in record time, too.

My mum has only recently confided in me about how much flak she had to put up with when *Puberty Blues* was published. I hadn't told her about the manuscript or shown her any of the content – it was so raw and racy. But apparently she received anonymous phone calls and letters berating her for having such a scandalous daughter and telling her she wasn't fit to be a teacher. You must remember that the generation gap was Grand Canyon-wide at the time and parents had no inkling of what their kids were really getting up to – the drugs, the sex, the drinking. That older generation was so easily scandalised. My poor parents needed to strap some shock absorbers to their brains. I'm sure there were rows and rows of raised eyebrows when they attended their respective churches each week – Mum was Anglican and Dad was Catholic – but they kindly kept that from me.

Both my mum and dad were products of wartime – frugality was in their nature. Plus there were no handouts. My mother's father was a bus driver and my father's father was a policeman. My parents were determined to make a better life for their family, and, as they both worked, they banked my mother's salary and lived on my father's wage. This meant that we could eventually afford a built-in swimming pool. That was a luxury. Most people had an above-ground Clarke pool. We also eventually had a rumpus room – the height of architectural chic. When I was twelve they took their long-service leave and we headed off around the world, in a campervan, all four girls packed in like sardines. It was the most exciting adventure, although we whinged to them much of the time about how much we missed our boring friends and how much we wanted to go home for a battered sav and a lamington, ungrateful brats that we were.

We lived in London for five months and went to Peckham Girls Comprehensive School – it was terrifying, like a minimum security high school – before traveling all over Europe, from Portugal to Turkey, via Italy, Switzerland, Greece, then on to America. We drove from New York to San Francisco, through hurricanes and tornadoes and dust storms and heat waves. It was so courageous of them, when I look back. I wouldn't bloody well do it now. Dad did all the driving and navigating – and all without sat nav – while Mum conjured up three meals a day from the tiny gas ring and washed all our undies in that tiny sink.

My parents brought us up to either work or study. When I did leave school, to become a hippy first and then a punk, squatting in a terribly run-down terrace in Woolloomooloo, I had every awful job going. I emptied bedpans in a hospital (hence the toilet humour, right?), I waitressed, made bathplugs in a factory, transplanted seedlings in a nursery – you name it,

I've done it. Nothing inspires you more in life than a bad job. I sold underwear at Woolies to old ladies and I kept thinking: 'I know I'm smarter than this.' So when I was seventeen or so I went on to get a column in the newspaper, and then published my first book (co-written with a girlfriend) by age nineteen.

I'm not really motivated by money, but with my parents' stories of the Depression and the war shortages soaked into my psyche, I do like to be secure. I love to look around and think: 'I bought all of this with wit and words.' I actually wrote this house. My gorgeous apartment in Potts Point, overlooking Sydney Harbour, is entirely bought from my book royalties. And that's a good feeling.

Much to my mother's horror, I'm not frugal. I follow Oscar Wilde's mantra that if you take care of the luxuries, the necessities will take care of themselves – so I'm always pouring champagne down my friends' necks and taking them out to swing from chandeliers.

I think my Mum and I must look very alike. Women would often stop me on the local Hurstville bus and say: 'You must be Val Grieve's daughter!' I hope I do look like her, as she's so lovely – to me anyway. We share a love of laughter. Mum's humour is drier than an AA clinic. She's also Wikipedia with a pulse, and a walking thesaurus and dictionary. During family Scrabble, we all defer to her as the oracle.

Personality-wise, I just wish I could be more like her. My sisters and I can't get over how selfless and kind and thoughtful she is. Whenever I stay with her – and she's well into her eighties now – she gets up in the morning to cook my breakfast and squeeze my orange juice and walks a few miles to the shops to get my favourite fish for dinner. Plus she's the world's best grandma to her eight grandkids who also all adore her. I don't think any woman really appreciates all the sacrifices her mum made for her until she is making the same sacrifices for her own kids. The sleepless nights, always taking the burnt chop, the knowledge that you would take a bullet for them without a moment's thought. Plus, seeing your mum laughing and playing and delighting in her grandchildren gives you an extraordinary window into the past, because this is how she was with you. It's the most nourishing feeling.

I do feel guilty about my teen years. I was a truly terrible teenager. As soon as I got taken hostage by my hormones, I turned into Attila the teen. I'd been school captain and sports captain and starred in the school musicals and been top of the class – but then I transmogrified overnight into a surly, snarly, boy-obsessed malcontent. Mum tried every strategy – kindness, crossness, grounding me, reasoning, restraining. All failed miserably. I think at one time there was even talk of sending me off to a school for uncontrollable girls. But luckily, love won out.

Mothers and their teenage daughters have more wars breaking out on a daily basis than the Balkan States. Teenage daughters seem to have an 'I find my mother contemptible' clause written into their contracts. The biggest area of conflict with my own mum was boyfriends.

When my own daughter went through her terrible teens, it helped to remember all the grief I'd made my own poor mama endure – all those years of eye-rolling, third-degree sarcasm and Neanderthal boyfriends with three-grunt vocabularies.

The truth is, besides feeding and watering and prodding with a foot occasionally to see if it's still alive, there's no foolproof method of raising a teenager. But the joyful news is that they do come through it. By twenty-one I'd re-emerged, full of love, light, laughter and devotion to my darling mother, as did my own daughter – although, when she went a tad feral and momentarily rejected me during her teen years, I did allow my mum a little light gloating.

By the way, my top parenting tip: if a rabid teenage daughter does get loose in your home, do not under any circumstances approach it. This creature is armed and dangerous. It has teeth. Back slowly out of the house and sleep on the nature strip. And if it ever screams at you: 'I wish you'd just die!' take a big gulp of wine and a drag on your fag and simply reply: 'I'm doing my best, darling.'

What I learned from my Mum is:

Don't sweat the small stuff.

You're of pioneering stock.

Nobody can make you feel inferior unless you let them.

Laugh and the world laughs with you, cry and your martini gets salty.

I wish I'd inherited her ability to cook the perfect cupcake. But I'm so, so glad I don't have her terrible singing voice. I keep thinking it will turn into a tune, but it doesn't.

One big difference is that my mother's generation didn't like to talk about sex and relationships. There was some brief, cursory chat when I was twelve which involved awful sanitary towels with belts, but apart from that it was the mother-daughter film at school. Ugh, do you remember those films? It's a wonder the Pope isn't ringing us up for tips on celibacy.

My generation tried to be the opposite. We want to talk about every nuance of sex and relationships and mucous viscosity. Of course, our daughters react to this with horror. My darling daughter only wanted to use the word 'period' if it was next to the word 'Jurassic' or 'Hellenic'. It makes me laugh now to think how teenagers would rather die than be seen in public with their parents. My own daughter went through that stage. Living with a teenage daughter is like living with a little dictator – you're not allowed to laugh, sing, dance, wear short skirts or be seen in a ten mile radius of your child!

My husband has never said to me: 'You're just like your mother.' And if he did say that, it would be a compliment. He's more likely to say: 'Can't you be more like your mother?' What I covet is her patience. I'm of the 'instant gratification takes too long' school of thought. I also covet her deep kindness – Mum always gives people the benefit of the doubt and sees goodness in all.

The trouble with our mum is that she made it all look so easy. Having a big family of funny, raucous, boisterous kids seemed the most natural thing in the world to me. It never occurred to me not to want children. And then when the snooze alarm went off on my biological clock, I thought I'd breeze through it all, just like Mum. I definitely had days where I wanted to put my kids back into the condom vending machine for a refund. The great thing about being a writer is that it's cheaper than therapy. I turned all that angst into a comic novel called *Mad Cows*, which was made into a film staring Joanna Lumley.

If there were an Olympic medal for grandmothering, Val would win gold. She is the best grandma in the world. She has eight grandchildren – all four of us had two kids each – and she has partly raised them all. She's let them beat her at dominos and cards and destroy her house to build forts and cover her in green make-up and glitter, which she's occasionally forgotten about and worn to church.

My mother is so young at heart, it's hard to believe that she's now a widow in her eighties. When my darling dad died suddenly from blood clots, we were devastated. Even though I'm an independent, feminist career woman in my fifties, I just felt like a little girl in desperate need of her darling daddy. It was only when he passed away that we truly understood how vital he was to our stability and happiness. He'd been our rock.

My mum and dad were passionately in love their whole lives. They met just before she left for London. Dad saw her off at the docks in Sydney – then drove all night like a bat out of hell to be waiting for her ship in Melbourne. She must have been gobsmacked with delight. Then, when her ship left port, he drove his old clapped-out jalopy all the way to Adelaide to wait on the dock again. A month or so later, he broke his collarbone in a game (Dad was a front row forward for the Canterbury-Bankstown Bulldogs) and couldn't play for while. His idea of convalescence was to follow his heart to England to continue their courtship. It's practically a rom-com.

I really do think that it's not until you have your own babies that you fully appreciate your own mother. You experience first-hand all the sleepless nights, the caring and mollycoddling, sticking out your hand in restaurants so your baby can spit out some offending vegetable, unknotting pee-stained shoelaces with your teeth – all the things she once did for you. Clearing up the vomit of the little creature whose poop is also leaking up its back, you think to yourself: 'My mother did this for me once.' The delayed gratitude washes over you, as it does each generation. Looking back, I don't know how my mother juggled everything, but she managed to combine kids and career at a time when not many women did so.

My mother's warmth and compassion really saved my sanity when my son was diagnosed with autism when he was three. This is a diagnosis which drags you into the dark. My darling boy had become a plant in a gloomy room and it was my job to drag him into the light. But I couldn't have survived that bleak, terrible time if I hadn't been able to confide in my Mum.

Mothering a child on the autism spectrum – well, it's kind of like trying to put together a giant jigsaw puzzle without the benefit of having a coloured picture on the box. There is no owner's manual. It's like finding a baby under a spaceship and bringing him up as your own.

My dear little boy had walked and talked early. He was so bright, advanced even. Then at about fourteen months he just suddenly lost his language. I'd presumed he simply had a chronic case of glue ear or some other minor ailment, so the word 'autism' slid into me like the sharp cold edge of a knife.

I can remember sitting in that doctor's waiting room in shock. He'd reduced my cherished child to a black and white term. But to me, my little boy was full of the most vibrant colours. I felt disbelief, followed by dismay and then a fiercely protective lioness-type love.

Denial is a common response of parents in my situation, so there were years and years of alternative medical rounds, trudging through a labyrinth of social workers, speech and occupational therapists and top pediatric psychologists. For years I trekked here, there and everywhere, in the endless search for experts. My son had so many tests, he must have thought he was being drafted into the elite astronaut program. And Mum was with me every step of the way, often pouring alcohol.

I hate to think how many doctors' children I have now put through university! Social workers were always telling me that being the mother of a child with special needs would be a challenge, but an exciting one. This is about as accurate as the captain of the Titanic telling his passengers that they were in for a diverting dip in the briny. But at least with Mum we could laugh at the more ludicrous moments and drink gin at the sadder times. And she took him for a few weeks a year so my husband and I could escape – go lie on a beach somewhere, sip cocktails with umbrellas in them and read inferior fiction.

The social isolation was so hard at times. The parent of a child with special needs suffers from creeping loneliness. I used to call the playground sandbox the quicksand box, as other parents, fearing some kind of leprosy-like contagion, would abandon my son and me, leaving only a numbing silence. Unusual behaviour is so often criticised by teachers and shop owners as bad parenting, with a crisp reprimand that you've obviously raised a 'spoilt brat'. Parents of kids with special needs too often just suffer in silence. I don't know how I would have survived all those bleak, emotionally draining, confusing years without the love, wit and warmth of my family. They accepted my quirky, brilliant boy for who he was and celebrated his differences. My family and I now know that there is no such thing as normal and abnormal. Just ordinary and extraordinary.

What I've learned from Mum and Dad is that friends and family keep you young. A gathering with my three sisters is nature's penicillin and so much cheaper than therapy. The other way to stay young is to never, ever turn down an adventure – which is why Mum and all four of us girls are planning a river cruise in France next year.

I've bought five tiaras, five berets and five captain's hats. No doubt we'll have to be hospitalised from hilarity. Those French had better bloody well look out. And if they annoy us in any way, we can always get Mum to sing.

ROBIN BOWLES

Her reputation as Australia's queen of crime has more to do with the release of various non-fiction book titles than with any personal wrongdoings. The former PR consultant turned to a career as an investigative writer in 1996 and is currently working on a new book. Life with her mother wasn't always rosy but her mother's passion for social climbing did teach Robin the joy of entertaining, which is now one of her great loves.

M y mother was a child of a couple who divorced in 1925, I think, so she was about four or five at the time. It was a very unusual thing, and she lived with her mother – my grandmother – and her grandparents.

They didn't want her around because she was too young and they all had lives, and my grandmother had to work in 'a home for retired gentlewomen' in Lilydale, so they sent her off to be a boarder at St. Catherine's in Toorak. And so there she was – a weekly boarder in a church school, daughter of divorced

Pictured: Rodney Coleman (Moir) in 1945

parents and her family lived just down the road. She felt very miserable about that. I track my mother's personality going right back down to that stage. She was very afraid of being rejected, so she became very assertive and selfish. She was very self-centred as well, and a dreadful snob.

She didn't talk much about that time, but I remember she did tell me that her grandmother gave her a box of biscuits once and she took them to the school but because she was a fat little girl – quite chubby – the nuns took the box away and she wasn't allowed to have them and she cried. She also told me that if she ever wet the bed, they beat her. The only other thing she said was how difficult it was not having a father and being in a school where all the girls had a father and a mother.

My grandfather was a collector of Australian first edition books. He had a place in in Bridge Road in Richmond, and he used to hold these Friday afternoon drinks and get-togethers and had all sorts of people coming through. I remember my grandmother saying to me that she just got so tired of these 'ugly bohemian people' coming every Friday afternoon, putting their dirty boots on her coffee table. I am sure that's not the reason they split up, but I think that my grandmother, mainly, was always conscious of position and thinking of how people looked at you – that nouveau riche attitude people had in those days if they were becoming social climbers.

My mother didn't have much to do with her father for years and until I was eleven she'd hardly seen him at all – but then we got to know him quite well.

One of the very early memories of my mother is of me sitting at the kitchen table, being forced to eat my porridge – I hate porridge. My mother was forcing it in my mouth with a spoon and I was spitting it out. In the end, she said: 'Get down, get out of my sight,' and I thought I'd got out of it. That was breakfast. Then it was lunch and out came the same porridge, and dinner was the same porridge too. She used to do that quite a bit. She taught me if you like something, eat up and speak up, if you don't, eat up and shut up.

I was supposed to like my mother – she was my only mother – but I had this conflict all the time about not liking her because she wasn't always very nice. When I was upset and crying in my room, I'd think: 'I just want a proper mother,' because I saw other people and how their mothers behaved and my mother wasn't like that at all.

Mum probably didn't want us, but she was mad about Dad. Dad wanted children – I know that, and I know he was probably hoping for a boy, but my mother popped out two girls.

Whenever my mother used to talk about having me, it was always things like: 'You nearly killed me.' She said: 'You were such a big baby and were a breech birth and I had to be in the hospital for days and the nurse dropped a swab on the floor and then she put it on me and I got sick and I nearly died.' And I should have been Roger, not Robin! It was never a happy story. It always seemed like it was my fault and I'd just been a nuisance to her.

My mother was very interested in my father's progression in the army and she learned very quickly what an officer's wife needed do to be a good army wife. She worked hard at that and she was good at it. Everywhere we went, Dad moved up the ladder. He was Captain and then he was promoted to Major and we went to London for four years just after my sister was born, where he worked for MI6.

By the time we came back to Australia, dad was a Colonel and Mum was in her element being the CO's wife. She did morning teas at home and she made fantastic gem scones with butter – I loved those gem scones – and she'd have drinks parties too. People would come about six and have cocktails and I would pass around olives, wearing a pink nightie. I could read everybody's rank off their shoulder to offer the olives. At quite an early age, she taught me to eat fruit with a knife and fork, in case I was ever invited to Government House.

Mum held dinner parties where she'd invite people of influence and so I learned that entertaining was good – it was fun and a good way to bring people into your home. That's one way I am like her. My husband, Clive, and I entertain more than any of our friends we know. We have probably one or two dinner parties or lunch parties a month and then we have people at other times too.

My mother could be so nice and friends coming home from school with me would say: 'How can you say such horrible things about your mother – she is so lovely.'

But she was such a hypocrite. She would bring on Mrs Gorgeous while people were visiting and then, when people walked out the door, she'd say: 'Oh God, I can't stand that woman,' or: 'Oh, she's so common.' And she'd go on and on about it. I used to say: 'Why would invite her to your house if you don't like her?' And she said: 'I have to think of your father's position.' What she taught me in that little exchange was that I was never going to invite anyone into my house whom I didn't like.

I had a very conflicted relationship with my mother. My father's approval was very important to me and my sister – we were both in awe of him – and he expected us to love our mother and be good girls for our mother. He'd often say: 'How many times do I have to tell you do what your mother tells you?' It was just this ongoing juggle – wanting to get approval from my father for being nice to my mother but, on the other hand, she was never nice to us. You know, I can't remember a single time in my whole life that my mother put her arms around me.

There was a big age gap between me and my sister. There were times when we supported each other, but as we got older my sister started playing all those silly games that my mother used to play and so gradually I felt much more on the outside. I'm sure that's probably to do with a deficiency in my personality, in some ways – I am not blaming them entirely – but I just didn't feel that I was a part of the family for a long time.

Mum would say that I was clumsy, or I was fat, or even unattractive, or I didn't work hard enough at school. I used to come top in English, and I topped French and history, but because I wasn't very good at math it dragged down my overall average. So, I'd come home with this report card saying I was first in the class in English, first in French, first in Latin, but fourth in math and Mum would ask: 'What happened to the math?'

I was very insecure about who I was for many years and, in fact, it's only since I have been running my own business and certainly since I've started writing my own books that I feel that am a worthwhile person. I spent a lot of years thinking: 'Would Mum get upset if I did this?' Sometimes I'd do it anyway, to upset her!

Mum was little – five foot one – and my dad was six foot

three. She told me this lovely story about when they were out dancing after the war and he had his uniform on. There was this button on the breast with a tank on it, because he was in the Armoured Corps. She'd press into his chest and then when they'd finished dancing she had the imprint of the button on her forehead. I think that was one of the nicest stories my mother ever told me. They loved each other very much.

Their relationship probably didn't teach me a lot because I've been married four times. I never saw their relationship as the ideal relationship. I never saw them as the ideal couple that were meant for each other or anything like that, and my mother was always quite jealous about my father. She loved him, you know, but she was possessive as well.

It was a strange family and made more strange by the fact that we had to move every eighteen months or so because of Dad's job and start over somewhere else. So my mother would dive into these new communities with great gusto and create another group of women around her, but she never stayed anywhere long enough for people to get to know the real her because suddenly we were on the go again, off somewhere else. I think it suited her. I learned quite a lot about meeting new people from her.

Dad died when he was fifty-six. My mum was two years older than he was, so she was a widow at fifty-eight and she'd lost the person she adored. That was the only time in our whole relationship that I had some genuine admiration for her, because she carried on – she was absolutely devastated by it, but she picked herself up and she went to the Red Cross meetings and National Trust and Ionian Club and she just got on with it.

After a couple years I said to her: 'Why don't you go on a

cruise, Mum?' She'd done lots of cruising and at first she didn't want to go, but I convinced her and off she went. At first I'd get these postcards from her saying: 'In Greece – last time I was here I was with Daddy,' and that sort of thing, but she eventually got a taste for travel again and started taking some fantastic trips around the world. It was good for her. I thought she had really fallen but she just picked herself back up and I admired that.

Before Dad died, I was with him in the hospital and he said: 'I want you to promise you'll look after your mother.' I said: 'Yes Dad, I'll look after my mother.' He said: 'Promise me.' I said: 'I promise you.' So all the interaction I had with my mother after my father died was as a result of that promise I made to him. If he had died without specifically asking me that, I probably would've had very little to do with my mother for the rest of my life.

Mum taught me how to sew. That was a good thing. By the time I was sixteen or seventeen I was making all my own clothes. I could see something in a magazine or Vogue pattern book and I could make it and wear it and it was quite professional – I was a good sewer, thanks to her. It gave me a feeling of achievement and it meant I could have clothes that I couldn't otherwise afford. Mum also taught me how to shop well. She was a great one for a bargain and she always had a real nose for where she might get things cheaply. She'd also walk four blocks to save five cents on a cauliflower and the one she bought would be covered with black spots – so she did also teach me that you get what you pay for.

Mum used to say 'no' a lot to us as kids.

'Can we go to the movies, Mum?'

'No.'

And you'd ask her why and she'd say: 'Because I said so.' So, that's one thing I learned – I was never going to say no to my children unless I had a really good reason, and if I had a really good reason, I would share that reason with them and I would tell them no means no. But the result is that most times I say yes. I learned from the way she used to make me feel about myself that I always wanted to be nice to my kids, instead of being angry at them and yelling at them. Sometimes it was difficult – at twenty-five I had four kids under the age of five and they were a lot of work.

At one point the kids and I actually went to counselling. Coming home from work I'd often find their school bags out in the hall – I'd trip over them – and I always felt bad that the first thing I'd say when I got home was: 'What are all these school bags doing in the hall?' and 'Put them away!' Instead of: 'Hi, darlings.' I felt terrible about that and I would go into the kitchen and say to myself: 'I am just like my bloody mother.' So we went and did some counselling and the counsellor asked the kids: 'What don't you like about your mother?' and they said to her: 'We don't like it when she yells at us.' Then she said to me: 'What don't you like about your kids?' and I said: 'Well, I am working full-time and all I want them to do is just to put their school bags in their room and put their lunch boxes on the bench – why can't they do that?'

So we started this thing, which was quite new back then, although a lot of parents do this now, I think – we had the star system. We had a big chart on the wall and they got a star every night if they did their little jobs they'd been set. Things like filling the dog's water, emptying the dishwasher or setting the table.

That gave me a chance to say: 'Yes, you can have an ice cream,' or 'Yes, you can go on that outing.' And the reason I did that was because I knew that, otherwise, I might turn into the mother who always yells and the mother who always says 'no'. It was a very important thing in my life not to turn into that person.

I think Mum was as tough as old boots but, you know, she pretended she wasn't. She was only very little so when she'd want to get something from the top cupboard, she would say: 'Oh, it's such a long way up there – I hope I don't fall off the ladder.' Then Daddy would come in and say: 'I'll get it for you, darling.' Or she'd say: 'Oh, I'm so cold – is there a window open somewhere?' and of course there was and Dad would get up and shut it.

Mum loved dogs. She always had dogs until towards the end when her last dog died and then she was on her own. I bought her one of those big stuffed Old English sheepdogs – like the ones kids win at fairs – and she used to take him to bed with her. When she died, I said to the funeral directors: 'I want him sitting at the foot of her coffin.' And then off it went to the fiery furnace with Mum.

When I became successful as a writer, Mum was very proud and she'd tell people all about me and would introduce me in this sweet little voice: 'My daughter, Robin – she's an author.' But it was too late. The damage was done.

She was really ready to die about two years earlier than she did, but she just couldn't give in. She was a fighter. Instead of giving up she'd fight some more – it was almost as if she kept coming back from the dead.

When she did die, I went to the funeral directors and I had to choose a coffin, which I had never done before. Of course, they showed me the most expensive ones first and I said: 'I am not spending lots of money on this coffin – not because my mother hasn't got a lot of money but because she'd have a fit if she knew that I spent money on something that's going to be burnt.'

So then he showed me this pine thing but I just couldn't bury Mum in cheap pine. I ended up choosing a pine one that was mahogany stained.

That was what she was about – appearance, you know. It didn't really matter if it was pine on the inside, but she wouldn't want anyone to think that on the outside. Then he said: 'What would you like your mum to wear?'

I hadn't thought about that at all and then he asked me if I wanted satin lining.

I said: 'What would I want that for? She's not going to lie in it for long.'

She was just a shrivelled up little darling, at that point, but I chose her favourite outfit – a 1970s, quilted leopard-skin jumpsuit, all-in-one, you know, wide legs. It was all pulled and faded because it had been around for so long but she always used to wear that as her favourite outfit so I knew it had to be the leopard-skin jumpsuit.

She also had this Persian lamb fur coat and I didn't want to inherit that because I knew what they did to the little baby lambs so I gave them that to dress her in as well. I told them to make sure she had her teeth in – she would be mortified to go anywhere without her teeth – and I told them to leave her wedding ring on and all the bracelets that she loved to wear.

Then I got a call from the funeral home saying: 'You didn't bring any shoes.' I told them: 'Oh, she can have bare feet.' I mean, she wasn't going to know the difference.

My sister was furious when she found out I'd put the fur coat with her – she implied I might have stolen it. People get really funny about material possessions at times like that. But it went with her.

My sister came down before the funeral and I said: 'Would you like me to organise the flowers?' I knew the flowers Mum loved and I already knew a florist who would do a good job, but my sister said, 'I want freesias.' Mum died in March and the florist told me they couldn't do freesias at that time of year. I told my sister this, but she still said: 'I want freesias.' 'Well,' I said, 'if you want them, you'll have to organise it yourself.'

I ordered a wreath like Princess Diana had – a wreath of pink roses. Mum loved roses, so I did roses and my sister organised hundreds of freesias to be flown in from Singapore – she had married a millionaire – so there was this grand arrangement of freesias on top of the coffin and then these little pink ones from me.

Dad's ashes had been scattered in the bay when he died in 1978 and Mum wanted the same – same place – because she thought he might still be down there somewhere. We went out in this boat – my sister and her husband and their twin girls and me and my twin boys and my husband, Clive. We sat at opposite ends of the boat and out we went with the lawyer who had something like a milk carton with Mum's ashes in it.

When it came time to do the ashes, the lawyer took the lid

off and he tipped the ashes off the side of the boat. It was quite windy and as he tipped the ashes over, tossing Mum into the water, my sister said: 'I don't see any lumps there – where are the bracelets? Did you take those bracelets, Robin?' And I told her: 'I did not take the bracelets – I told the funeral people to keep them on.'

Then my sister said: 'There seems to be an awful lot of her,' and because Mum was so little, she said to the lawyer: 'Are you sure you've got the right container?' And my son, who is a chronic stirrer, said: 'Oh, don't worry about it, it's probably all the bloody freesias.' So my sister got really upset and she stormed off to the back of the boat, and just then the boat turned around. This gust of wind came up and the last of Mum's ashes just blew back all over us – in my eyes, in my hair, all over my clothes. Everywhere.

Clive just looked at me and said: 'She's going to have the last word isn't she?' My sister missed it all because she went to the back of the boat in her tantrum about the freesias and I was left, on this boat in the middle of the sea, brushing Mum off me. Mum would have liked that.

GREG FLEET

Greg Fleet's childhood in Geelong was far from
normal. In his memoir, *These Things Happen*,
the comedian and actor shares the story of how
his father faked his own death, then turned up
years later, and of his mother battling on as a
single mother. He's a father himself these days
and if his mother has taught him anything, it's a
determination to help his own daughter grow up in
an environment where she feels secure and loved.

A fter her husband had lied to her, fucked other people
and faked his own death, he came back and managed to
convince Mum to take him back. That says a lot about who
she was. Regardless of all the horrendous things he'd done,
whether she admitted it or not, she remained in love with him.

I don't know if that means she was a weak person – I think
it means she was desperate to be loved. She would never have
admitted it but she spent her whole life wanting to be loved, and
the way that desperation came across made her a very difficult

Pictured: Greg Fleet's mother Sally Fleet, age four

person to be around for long periods of time. She could be very critical and snappy. She could also be absolutely hilarious.

She was born into a dodgy family where the kids were taken away by the state. She was put into an orphanage and then adopted by one of the wealthiest families in the state. They were very devoted to her, but then they split up. My mother stayed with her father and they had a fun life together for a couple of years, but when he remarried it became the classic evil stepmother story – his new wife had her own daughter from another marriage and she sort of shut my mother out.

Mum was born into a loveless situation, taken away, adopted, shown love, had that taken away again – and then she met my father. Her family realised he was a bit of an operator and they told her not to marry him, but Mum said: 'No, I'm going to – he loves me.' She was constantly being shown love – or something close to it – and then having it taken away. That was the story of Mum's life.

She and my father were born and raised in the United States. When he got transferred out to Australia because of his job with Ford, she just followed along. I guess it was a chance for a new life. There was no real family connection for her back in the US.

As a mother, she always came across as more like one of our friends. She wanted to hang out with our friends. That was okay because she was funny and kind of cool to be around but while I say that, it was never quite right. Even at my wedding, she didn't want to sit with my wife's family. She said, 'I don't want to sit with those old people.'

'But Mum,' I said, 'you're older than they are.' It was like she didn't realise.

The danger of being matey with your kids is that it takes away the ability to be what would be considered a proper mother.

I mean, she always made sure we had what we wanted and she always stood up for us and defended me against the horrendous paedophiles at Geelong Grammar, but maybe there was too much of that and not enough of being a rock for us to lean on.

Her acting that way – that wasn't so much of a thing until Dad had gone. I didn't really notice it before he left. Once he was gone, we kind of took the place of him – we became her confidantes as well as her children.

When I was a kid I once observed Mum telling my sister the story about my dad, and then I watched my sister kind of lose it. My sister was always very strong and when I saw her freak out and start crying – she is two years older than me, so she was about twelve at the time – I realised something fairly serious had gone down. I don't remember Mum addressing it with me, although I'm sure she must have at some point.

I don't know how long Mum really thought the story that he had committed suicide was true – but that's what we were told. In hindsight, looking at that situation, I think a large part of her would have been going: 'Hang on, he's pulled a shifty.' She knew a lot about him by that stage and he wasn't the suicidal type. I don't know how long she really thought it was true – it was probably the most comforting thing to believe. I think she wanted it to be true because it meant he hadn't rejected her – he had rejected life. I felt for her enormously that someone would do that to her. I felt for both of them that it came to that.

I remember her having a fight with me once – I was about

twelve – and her telling me that it was my fault that he had gone. I was recently talking to my sister about it and Mum had said the same thing to her, so that was clearly one of her weapons. She wanted someone to blame, other than herself.

There was a time when a kid at school had a crack at me about it – saying that I had no dad – and it was the first time that I felt that it was somehow shameful and embarrassing that we didn't have Dad around. But as I got older I met heaps of kids from single parent families and I realised it wasn't really anything to be embarrassed about.

The difference was to do with the way it all happened, with Dad pretending he had suicided and actually disappearing – and then being found by Mum to still be alive. Another difference had to do with the relationship between my mother and me. Someone said to me once that my mother had two modes of being – she could either be completely hilarious or she was absolutely furious but there was nothing in between. That was the difficult part.

Dad never gave Mum a cent from the moment he left, which must have been so hard for her. Not even a hundred bucks. He just totally absolved himself of all responsibility. It is a terrible thing to do to your children and to a woman who loved you, but I can also sort of understand that feeling of just waking up one day and realising you've made a terrible mistake and just wanting to get out. I can understand what that feeling must be like – 'This isn't my life. I've got to go.'

I was exposed to so much indulgence for the first ten years of my life and then suddenly my father was gone and it was taken away. We went from having everything to having nothing very quickly. I think I always resented my mother for not being richer than she was, which is a terrible thing. It's an easy trap to fall into – you're at a school where all your friends are loaded and their parents are loaded and you're facing that question about why you have to be the one who's got the shitty little yellow fibro cement house in Torquay. A more mature child might have handled it better but I kind of resented her. It's a terrible thing to admit to – resenting someone who goes out of their way to look after you and provide for you as best they can, for not being able to provide you with more.

I don't remember Mum telling me that Dad was actually still alive. In my memory, it was a teacher at school who pulled me aside and said: 'Your father's been found and he's coming here to see you.'

When he came out to the school and saw me I thought maybe he'd be this crazy, left-wing nut-job who'd been travelling around the world doing all these interesting things – this kind of amazing Dennis Hopper fugitive-like character – but it turns out he wasn't that at all. He was this right-wing, racist, gun-loving homophobic embarrassment – typical American right-wing nutter.

I didn't think it was a good idea that Mum let him come back. He was back and trying to be a father and telling me what to do but I wasn't having it. He and Mum started fighting again and it was just like before he left – hearing them late at night just constantly niggling at each other. I was just thinking: 'What are you doing?' We'd already played that record and nobody liked the tune.

I think it taught me to be pretty crap at relationships, too.

I love the people I love – I love them very deeply. I've been in love quite a few times in my life – more times than you're meant to be – but I never really learned the right limits and how you're meant to treat people to keep them around. I learned how to treat people to make them fuck off.

Mum and I used to have the most horrendous arguments. I was taught to fight in such a way that you would say the cheapest, meanest, most destructive things you could as quickly as possible in an effort to win the argument. We would say the most horrifying things to each other, and then five minutes later we'd be like: 'Do you want a coffee?'

So I took that with me into relationships – with girls, with friends, with anybody – and as I did that to people I could actually see them shut down. I remember a couple of girlfriends ending relationships because they could not believe some of the things I would say and do to them. I would say the most personal, hurtful thing I knew about them – really awful. But then ten minutes later, I'd be like: 'Hey, do you want to go into the city and do this or that?' The girls would be like: 'What? What are you talking about? I don't want to be anywhere near you.' And I didn't understand.

I'd been brought up to think that was normal, but I know now it's not normal. It's not normal at all. It's something that is really damaging and really scarring and it's a sign of someone who's had a really dysfunctional life.

Mum was like that with all of us kids. Before she died, Mum was at a home in Geelong and she wasn't doing too well for a long time. It was interesting and weird, too – because her brain cancer actually made her easier to get along with. She wasn't as judgemental as she used to be.

She used to say things just to push my buttons. I remember once, about fifteen years ago, we were having one of our usual horrendous fights and I said: 'Wait, wait, let's just let it go this time. Before we do this, let's just talk like people who love each other and are trying to communicate, rather than doing what we normally do.' I could see, just for a few seconds, that she was going to do it and it was going to be this great breakthrough moment in our lives – and then she just went: 'Oh God, what are you – some kind of hippie?' She couldn't do it. It was such a shame because I was sure that in this moment we were finally going to communicate. We were right on the edge of something, then she just went: 'Nup.'

There's a habit in our family of playing the victim, so it's always hard to know what's true and what's an exaggeration. When Mum told me things about her childhood, I had to balance out what was actually fact and how much of it was wanting to be a victim. And it wasn't just her – we all do a bit of that in my family.

I had empathy and sympathy for her. I mean, she probably made it worse for herself in a lot of ways but this was a woman who had a really hard life. So many times she came close to having it all sorted out, but then it fell apart again. I had to eventually get to the point where, when I went to see her, I'd be a little quieter than I used to be. I tried not to get too emotionally involved. I knew, by then, that she'd say and do things that would stir me and I used to get pushed to the point where I would go: 'Fuck you – how can you say that?' More recently, I'd just let it go.

I had to become the adult, and it was one of the few mature things I've ever done. I finally worked out that she wasn't going to change – she wasn't going to change for me or for anyone. I got to the point where I let her say and do what she wanted and

I found that, because I stopped reacting the way I used to, she didn't go as far as she used to. She no longer got the reaction she wanted.

The fact that Mum managed to get three children through their education and into the world is pretty cool. Here was a woman who was completely isolated on the other side of world from her family with three children. I don't know why she didn't go back to the States when Dad left. That's what I would have done. I would have thought: 'I've got nothing here – I need support,' and I would have gone back to America and leant on my family. But she didn't. Through stubbornness or whatever, she thought: 'No, I'm staying here and that's that.'

There are all kinds of good things I learned from her: a sense of humour, a sense of confidence in the world, an attitude to not be intimidated. She could be a very funny person at times – we all laughed a lot growing up, despite everything else.

Certain things would upset me. Mum never wanted the neighbours to hear us fighting. She liked to keep things private. I was writing a letter to my girlfriend once and she said: 'Never put anything in writing that you wouldn't want to see on the front page of the paper.' I was like: 'Wow, that's a bit full-on.' I wouldn't have cared if anyone had put the things I was writing about on the front page of the paper because they were true. The fact that she was worried about whether the neighbours would hear us fighting annoyed me and years later I wondered why she wasn't more worried about the fact that *we were fighting*. It would have made more sense to me if she'd said: 'Hey, let's stop fighting,' rather than: 'Hey, let's fight quieter.'

I don't want to sound like I've been too harsh on my mum. I know I learned a lot from her. I can't put my finger on exactly what all those lessons are but when I look at the way I've lived my adult life – which has been a catastrophe, in many ways – maybe I didn't learn enough. I think a lot of things I did learn – and I'm sure many people in my generation would feel the same way – were kind of more about what *not* to do.

I think Mum was embarrassed about many of the things I've done. She used to say: 'Why do you want to focus on acting?' until I was finally on TV and then she was like: 'My son, the actor.'

I am sure this might be a bit self-indulgent but when it came to the drug stuff I always felt like her thoughts were more about what people would think, rather than about my welfare. That annoyed me. I never felt it was coming from a place of: 'Oh my God, my son's involved in something that could kill him,' but that it was more about: 'My son is involved in something that will reflect badly on the way I brought him up.'

I think Mum did the same thing many parents did. She'd ask: 'Are you still taking heroin?' and I'd say: 'No.' I mean, I was never going to say yes. But I never felt that she was asking because of her really strong need to protect me.

For me, reality has always been a bit of a rude shock. I came to my own conclusions about things and they'd always been romanticised idylls of out-there, crazy, rebellious men or strong, passionate, independent women and – in the end – people are none of those things. People are a little bit of that but they're a little bit something else too – they're a combination of all sorts of things.

I was always a bit disappointed that Mum let Dad back into our lives. I didn't know what to do with a father. I didn't know how to behave – were we meant to kick the footy together? I mean, she was better at that stuff than he was, anyway. I will give her that. She really went out of her way to do sport, drama – whatever we were into. I worked out that the only way to get her approval was to succeed at something in the eyes of other people.

Actually, I suspect maybe that's one of the reasons why I became a performer. You get instant gratification from performing before a large number of people you don't know. You stand in front of an audience and they are immediately responding – and hopefully saying 'yes' – and giving you that approval. With Mum, I'd go through all this junkie madness but as soon as I'd be on *The Flying Doctors* or something all would be forgiven because Mum would be able to tell her friends that I was on TV, or doing some interview or whatever.

I've never blamed either of my parents for my situation. A lot of my friends have said: 'Oh, you probably ended up having a drug problem because your father left.' Maybe that is true to some degree, with regards to things both of them have done, but I certainly don't blame them for the choices I've made.

Mum and I hardly spoke from about the time my daughter, Sunday, was born, until not long before she died. I found it strange that she wasn't more interested in her granddaughter. We'd go down to visit her and she'd go on about herself, never asking my daughter anything about her life. I think grandmothers are meant to dote on their grandchildren and they're meant to ask them how they're doing, you know: 'How's school?' But when I went to visit not long before she died, there were pictures of Sunday up on her wall – I didn't get it.

I think I felt that I wasn't prepared for being a dad and I didn't know how to be a parent. Most of the good parenting in my daughter's life comes from her mother, who is a remarkable person. Fortunately, we're really close. There were a few years when we really hated each other but we've come through that to a new place where we are great friends.

A lot of my daughter's wellbeing comes from her mother – not from me. I feel guilty that I haven't been a great parent. I haven't been terrible but I haven't been the best, and I'm trying now, as much as I can, to be with my daughter and leave a legacy for her. We've hardly ever fought, my daughter and I. We see each other every other day when I'm in Melbourne, and when I'm not, we talk on the phone.

She'll often get really emotional and upset when she misses me while I'm away, but then when I'm around, she's really cool. It's like she doesn't want to show me any vulnerability. Maybe she thinks I'll run away – which is terrible. She became very upset when she realised I had a drug issue because I guess she was terrified that maybe I would die. She'd never say that to me. So I'd sit her down and say: 'Look, that's in the past.' She seems pretty stoic but I don't think kids should be stoic. They're kids.

I think one of the things I've gained through my own relationship with my Mum is that I've tried to do it differently with my daughter. I've tried to create a situation where we can talk about what we're feeling and it's okay if we have differences of opinion.

You have to step up and be an adult when you're a parent. I never want to be that father who says: 'Well, if you're not going to call me, I'm not going to call you.' I'll be the one just to pick up the phone and ring and say: 'Hey, how's it going?'

I will always say that Mum did a remarkable job in many ways. She managed to keep going and give us what we needed to get by, and on that level she was a remarkable woman. I don't envy her life at all – I think she had a really tough life. I think she made it harder on herself along the way but she still did an incredible job and I did love her very much. Unfortunately, there were things that were definitely not ideal but that is the case in lots of mother-child relationships, I guess.

It's easy for comedians to talk about dysfunction in families. It certainly is a good source of material because everyone understands it.

Mum was a really funny woman. Serious things would happen at school and we'd be in trouble with one of the teachers and she would deal with them in a serious way but then, a few minutes later, she'd make some crack about the teacher involved and we'd all be laughing. I do remember that. Growing up, there was a lot of laughter. We laughed a lot. That was pretty cool. I do appreciate that.

There's a photo of Mum when she was a little girl and she'd just been adopted. You can see joy in her eyes but also fear – a fear that would transform over the years to a dark anger, relieved at random moments by a hilarious, lovely lightness. When she died, all of her pain and anger ceased. I think I feel relief.

MIGUEL MAESTRE

Miguel Maestre was born in Murcia, Spain. He
decided to make Australia home and enjoys life in
Sydney with his wife and young children. As the co-
host on Channel Ten's *The Living Room*, he dishes
up his culinary delights to a national audience,
and the cookbooks he produces take his flavours to
kitchens all around the world. When Miguel thinks
of his mama and the way she handled life with
three very active sons, he has one burning question:
How did she do it?

To be honest, I was a full-on child. Very outgoing. Very
confident. Very loud. My other two brothers, Carlos and
Antonio – they were more quiet. Of the three of us, I made my
mama work the hardest. I look back on that now and wonder
how she did it.

Like all parents, mine really wanted me to find the right
direction when I was young. It was obvious I was really
outgoing and I had a lot of friends, and I think because they

---

Pictured: Florentina Maestre

didn't know which way I was headed, they wondered what might happen to me. We were not a rich family – just average – but my papa always worked hard for us to go to the better schools. My brothers both got degrees from a good university, but I didn't have an interest in that kind of study. I was the one who was happy just being with my friends, playing sport and not focusing too much on my future. I wasn't very good at school – there was just too much fun going on elsewhere.

Mama was so patient with me. Her patience affected me in an amazing way because throughout my youth I didn't really know what goal to go after. I thought I wanted to be a chef, and because my mama told me all my life that I was good at cooking and had been so supportive, I had the motivation to just go for it. Mama always made me feel I could have a big dream and make it come true.

I told my mama and papa I wanted to go overseas and become a chef and Mama immediately supported it. I told them: 'I want to experience life, go to another country, learn English,' and they helped me do that. I was surprised in a way because it is quite scary for parents to have their child go to another country. But they let me. I was eighteen when I left home and in Spanish families that is very unusual. Normally, in Spanish families, everyone stays together for a long time.

Now that I've got kids, I don't know how I'll be. I am sure that, secretly, they must have been worried, but Mama never showed me that and because I knew they were happy for what I was doing, every little step I took – learning a new language, becoming a chef, and slowly getting better at what I was doing – they were always there for me, a hundred per cent.

The strength of who I am today is because of the support

that my mama – and my papa – gave me. It was one of the very important parts of my life. I would not have my success, my job, or even my family, if they had stopped me from doing what I believed in.

My memories of my mama are all really beautiful. Taking us to school, holding our hands, always being kind and loving us so much. She has always been very passionate about family because she comes from a huge family. Back in Spain, at one stage my mama had twenty siblings. Some of them died when they were just little babies and a couple of my uncles died later on, but there are still twelve brothers and sisters alive today.

I think she has got it in her blood a little bit – being a really good mother. Everything I remember of Mama is always just really wonderful – and there are many memories of her in the kitchen, cooking for us. She is a really good cook and she always cooked a lot of food for us. She would cook these amazing omelettes – thirty eggs and it would last three or four days for the whole family and I would ask her: 'How you do that?' or: 'Can I peel the potatoes?' The Mediterranean family is so much about food, and with the food comes the family, so I think Mama and I have got a great chemistry when it comes to food. She always raised us boys to know how to look after ourselves and she told me that I had better know how to cook some dinner. I always listened to what she said – but then I always ended up doing whatever I wanted.

Mama was also very serious about cleaning. That's something she passed on to me. I am a really tidy person. My mama always had us cleaning the house – just making it a beautiful place for all of us to be. When I'm cooking now at home, even before I finish cooking, all my dishes are spotless already and I've got the dishwasher waiting for more when we finish dinner. It's something I am very grateful for – these habits.

Mama was so good at home, and she was so organised with life. And sewing – she loved to sew. I remember her always changing the pillows on the sofa. She was so skilful. She would buy fabrics and sew them into new curtains, new pillow covers – our house always looked fresh and clean. I remember my jeans breaking and she'd fix them in no time, or I remember if a t-shirt had a little stain she was really good at just getting rid of it somehow. It was like magic, the things she used to do.

We always felt like she was there for us all the time but, really, she was doing so many other things too. Mama and Papa had a few shops and she was always cleaning, checking that there was enough stock to sell – she was so busy helping my papa run the shops on top of running the whole house, too. She never made it seem like she was too busy for us – she was always there when we needed her.

Mama still gives me advice and tells me what to do. That's what mothers do, right? It never stops – even when you grow to be a man. Yesterday, I was cooking dinner – I was making a quail and chorizo paella for dinner for all of us – and my mama was looking at me saying: 'Oh, Miguel, you should fry the rice first, or you should put this in, or that.' I said: 'Mama, are you going to tell me anything else? I am already a chef – I know how I like to cook paella.' But she said: 'No, no – *before* you were a chef, I told you how to do this, and now you are changing it.' In situations like this I always tell her that I am cooking one of my recipes, but she still will not give up – she says that I should have put the paprika in earlier. We have always had an amazing rapport and we still do. Sometimes, you just have to listen to your mother and not argue. It happens a lot. We will have these amazing conversations about the way to prepare food the 'proper' way. It's not a fight – never a fight – but Mama is happy to tell me what she thinks.

My mama's ambition? Simple – for us to be successful, for us to be happy. I think she is really happy now because we are all settled in a kind of really nice life in different ways. They never had expensive cars or expensive presents or expensive watches or anything like that. Their focus was on loving us. That's what my mama did so well. I think that has helped the three of us boys make better lives for ourselves – our ambitions are probably to show our parents that all their hard work actually paid off. My brothers and I are all happy and we have our own families and we do well and all of that is because of them. Mama, of course, but Papa as well. In that way, my mother's ambitions have been fulfilled.

Now I have a company that sells Spanish products to Australian supermarkets and it is my dream come true – to have all my family working together in one business.

My parents still live in Spain and I go there to see them when I can. When I was younger, I used to travel for ages all around the world – I went to a million places – but now, the older that I get, the more I miss my family every day. Having my own family is a big part of that – it makes you remember how important little things are. There are so many special things that come from being with people who know you and love you. My parents have been visiting this past week. They are staying with us for a month this time and I can already feel in my chest that those days are counting down. I already miss them and they have not left yet. Eventually, I would like to bring them here to live with us in Australia, but – who knows?

I think the key to being happy in life is finding that one thing – that thing that is yours. To do that, you must try the many tastes of life. Like when you are eating food – you don't know you like a cuisine until you try them all.

So what we are trying to do as parents is just have an idea that, if we let our children try sport, or let them try dance, or let them try music, or try painting, that one day they will identify with one thing that they love. I would give everything I have to help my kids follow their dreams – because my mama did the same for me when I was young.

Where I grew up in Spain, in Murcia, it is all beaches, like here in Sydney. Because we lived very close to the coast, Papa got a sailing boat and used to always take us sailing. My mama had her huge family and my papa had five brothers and sisters and there were always cousins and friends and grandparents – so many people, all the time. Someone would go hunting and Mama would cook some rabbits and my grandma would cook a huge paella – there were always so many people. Sunday lunch meant there was so much to do – so many plates to put out, so many big tables to sit down at.

We'd go and see the chickens at my grandfather's farm, go for a swim – with so many people around me, childhood felt like a big event, all the time. It was never just the five of us.

When I think of us growing up like that and then my family here in Australia, I am always trying to do that. I try to bring a little of my childhood from Spain into my Australian lifestyle on a daily basis, any way I can. So when my boy turned one year old, I put on a big birthday party and invited a hundred of my friends. People were like: 'Miguel, you invite all these people, do all these crazy things – I normally just have ten people.' But for me, the people – all my friends and people I love – are so important. It reminds me who I am and why I am here – and it reminds me of Mama. It's crazy and noisy, but that's how I grew up.

I speak Spanish to my kids, Claudia and Morgan. Claudia is already fluent – she can understand everything I say – and I try to keep different little Spanish customs happening in my family. I am also trying to keep using Skype with mama and papa so they can keep those Spanish roots alive for me and for my kids to grow up with.

In my house, there is not one day in the week that there are not four or five people for dinner. My sister-in-law lives next door and she comes for dinner, and my mother-in-law is very close and she comes for dinner, and my father-in-law lives close and he comes for dinner, too. I like to have my table full of people because the way I express myself is through my family and it makes me strong – it makes me the richest man in the world. I consider myself the richest man in the world because when I come home there are always people there – and it is beautiful.

That's another special connection between my mama and me – I have her name. My street name is Miguel Cascales Maestre. Cascales is my papa's surname and Maestre is my mama's surname, so I cut my name short when I went to Australia because the full Spanish surname is too long for my media career. Miguel Cascales doesn't sound as good as Miguel Maestre. Now it has a better flow, but in Spanish culture it is very funny not to have your papa's name. I asked my papa: 'Are you okay, are you sure that you don't mind?' My papa always jokes, and he says: 'I am going to start calling myself Antonio Maestre.'

So now my kids and my whole family will carry that surname forward from my mama, and that is really, really special – just so special.

People always try to think about who they are more like – their papa or their mama. In my family, I think both my brothers are more like my papa, but I am almost the double of my mama – she is always really happy and is a very family-oriented woman. My mama is also very strong. I've seen her crying only once or twice in my life. I remember my mama being very upset when my grandpa died.

When my mama comes here to visit and we go to the super-market, sometimes people stop and take photos of me and it makes my mama so proud. I understand it more and more now because I have got kids of my own. Being a parent is such a powerful feeling and I think, really, only now do I really understand how she feels. I would find it so hard to have my own kids living so far away – 17,000 kilometres from me – but I think it is actually making our relationship stronger because we know there are other things we are missing by not being in the same country together.

When you are an immigrant like me – it's hard to explain. Sometimes you feel Spanish, sometimes you feel Australian and sometimes you don't know what you feel because you've got so much of each culture – two lives apart in two very different places. It must be hard for my mama to understand, but I believe she is really proud that I embraced my Australian life in such a beautiful way with our home and our family. My kids are Australian, my wife is Australian and mostly I feel like a normal Australian guy – a normal bloke. But, I believe I am really a Spanish guy as well and my connection with Mama is a big part of feeling that way.

I always try to call Mama two or three times a week and because the show is not shown overseas, I always send all the links of everything we do and I try to keep the family updated.

Me having kids didn't change anything between my mama and me. I haven't started to see my mama as grandmother of my kids – I still see my mama as my mama.

To be honest, I haven't changed much from those early days. I have become a little more mature but I am still really full-on and really hyperactive – twenty-four hours a day. I think Mama would define me as a really, really active kid with a really big smile and always, always being really happy, always with a lot of friends.

I was the kid who would be trying to catch a snake, the one who would be going for the crazy things, the one running up the stairs, the one who would not be scared to do tricks on his bike, the silliest one, the loudest one, and the one who wanted to have the most attention.

I think it is very challenging in life to find a person who you can share your life with – all those years with – because you know every day is a different day. To find somebody you can spend all that time with is really hard, and my parents are lucky that they found each other. I think I am lucky that I did, too, and I'm just trying to live by their example. I wish everyday that when I am sixty, my wife, Sascha, and I are just and strong and happy as my mama and papa are.

The Spanish name for grandmother is *abuela*. I make sure I tell stories about her and keep her name within us, even when Mama is not here, so my children know her and remember her.

She is too young now, but when Claudia grows up she will understand that Abuela is Papa's mama. I cannot wait to go on holidays to Spain more often so she can see where I grew up, so she can understand, so I can tell her that Abuela and I did this and that when I was a kid, so I can show her another example of how a childhood can be lived. When you become a parent, looking back on your own life becomes even more important and has a bigger meaning. I am looking forward to all of that.

One of the proudest moments for my mama and Papa was when I was awarded the Spanish Order of Civil Merit for the work I am doing in the media to promote my country. When the Spanish newspapers called me and featured me, they asked me who my idol was – who I wanted to be when I was older. My answer was my papa.

Papa was really emotional when he read that in the Spanish paper. When I was a little boy, he never cried, but my mama said she saw him crying that day.

The impact for them is very big. They are both so proud, because they just can't believe it – they can see me on TV or in a magazine and they can see our products in supermarkets with my name on them, and it's a good feeling for them, that I achieved something.

Mama always says; 'Oh, Miguel you are the champion, you

did so well,' but it is the same with my other brothers too – she is a very good mama and she has that pride – that love – for all three of us in her heart.

I think she is really good at spreading her love, and very good at spreading encouragement. That's what great mamas do – they have a power that makes all their children feel special.

I think what I learned the most from Mama is how to be really happy and be really strong, and to have the strength to never give up on things. That has been one of the very best lessons. In the past, when I failed at something and would not want to try again, she would always say something to make me keep going – and that is when I would succeed.

I hope she feels she has done a good job. I truly believe she has.

Hopefully, one day, my kids will say the same about me.

LAWRENCE MOONEY

Lawrence Mooney traded his dreams of being a motor mechanic for the life of a performer – all thanks to his mum and a timely warning. His career has taken him from comedy clubs to radio studios and television screens. And now he has his own children, Lawrence looks forward to sharing his mother's wisdom with them.

'Make the bed and the whole house looks tidy.' Wisdom from Mum.

Going back a long time, I said to her: 'I want to act,' and she told me: 'Well, they're not going to come looking for you.' She was right about that.

I was a teenager – I think we were watching *Lawrence of Arabia* again – and I was like: 'Yeah, that's what I want to do. I want to be Peter O'Toole.'

I'd gone from wanting to be a motor mechanic for a long time – I was obsessed with cars – to wanting to be an actor, because my parents sat me down around at the age of eleven, and, I remember very specifically, said to me: 'You are not going to be a motor mechanic.'

'No?'

'No. Because that's not the life you want to live.'

My father was a mechanical engineer. He said: 'It is cold, it's dirty – you spend all of your life bending over or on your back.'

Mum said: 'You're not doing it.'

Dad said: 'You know, you can become rich doing other things and then you can have as many cars as you want.'

It was like they were telling me: 'We didn't come to this country so you can, you know, not evolve.'

Not that I want to talk down being a motor mechanic – that was just their attitude. They were from Liverpool in England. They came out in 1958, and they thought I needed bigger dreams.

I became obsessed with being a cop for a while, too. I didn't have a broad range. Mum and Dad didn't put me off that idea, specifically. That one just kind of petered out, and then showbiz caught my imagination. And that was that.

Mum's life philosophy when it came to a career was – and this might come from the fact that my parents lived through the war and were born during the Depression – 'You can only get so far with a bag of clothes, but you can go as far as you like with a bag of money.' She said: 'Do whatever makes you happy in life but always make sure you've got a lot of money.'

My father was always very frugal. You know, squeeze that toothpaste tube until it's got nothing left in it, then split it open and scrape out the rest. My mum's response was kind of the opposite – never have an empty cupboard. Every shelf full, fridge full, wardrobe full – make sure you've got plenty of money to give yourself all the things you want.

I was never going to sing or dance. I wasn't attracted to that kind of thing at all. And, to be honest, I could neither sing nor dance. So my mum said: 'You've got to go to the local amateur theatre company,' and I said: 'Theatre? I want to do movies.'

'No, no,' she said, 'this is how it is. All the greats – Richard Burton, Peter O'Toole – they all started on the stage and then graduated into films.'

That's how, in my late teens, I headed to the local amateur theatre company, then onto fringe theatre in the city and it kind of just kept going from there. As a kid, I loved watching Dave Allen on TV but I didn't know what to call that, you know. I didn't know there was such a thing as comedy. That was another discovery.

I had two older siblings and I think parents often allow the youngest to do what they want. I was born into the privileged position of being the baby.

I've done a lot of stand-up about this where, you know, the oldest has a lot of expectations put on them and responsibility. They're good solid people and then the middle child is the baby for a while but then they're the middle child and they don't want to follow the footsteps of the eldest, so they sort of fire off to the left somewhere and blaze their own trail and often go a bit crazy. I would say that's a good description of our family. And my brother, the middle child, might be a bit crazy but middle children have a charisma all of their own. He's an entrepreneur and employs forty-odd people and runs a big components company. Then there was me.

I did six years as a customs officer – I still had this thing for jobs in uniforms – and then I decided to go to South America. I trekked around there for six months with a friend, then came back gainfully unemployed, worked in the shipping industry for a while and then decided to quit and follow my dream. I didn't actually go to drama school – at The National Theatre in St Kilda – until I was twenty-seven.

All the way through that I did itinerant labour, so I worked as a debt collector and a window cleaner. Those were my last real jobs before I got a break on *Denise* back in 1999. I think I clean a good window. In fact, I look at windows all the time and go: 'Hey, good job.'

Mum allowed me to be a bit of an intellectual snob. My parents used to say: 'Always hang out with people better than yourself.'

'But what about them?' I would say. 'Will they want to hang out with me if they're better than me?'

And Mum would say: 'You know what I mean – aspire to be better than those around you, move yourself up.'

Mum was always about the finer things in life. She brought avocado into the house and cracked it open for the first time and we were all like: 'What are these things? They taste like soap.' It was weird.

I reckon that she wanted to go university and I think that getting married and then migrating cut those aspirations short. I think she was frustrated, but she worked in a professional position most of her life. She was the personnel manager for Adidas, which is what they called the human resources manager back then. And after fifteen years of doing that, she was fucked over – you can call it sex discrimination – and was replaced by a man who was paid twice the money. They changed the position title and doubled the wage – she knew it was happening.

Mum had been home with me full time until I was about eight. She loved being a mother – she just loved having three boys – but there came a point when she wanted to get back into it. And then, I think, the ambition to graduate burned in her all of her life. When she was finally finished with professional life she went to university, took up an Associate Diploma and finished with a BA. She went on to do honours in theology – she's always been a devout Catholic. She got a job doing pastoral care work with her church and was employed until she was eighty, but then the axe fell again. Being laid off at the age of eighty isn't exactly an insult – you're eighty, go and do something else – but she took it terribly, personally. She doesn't go easily, my mum – stubborn as fuck.

She would help people in palliative care organise the last weeks or months of their lives – whether it be six weeks or six months.

'Do you want to throw all your photos in an album or clean out the second drawer? Or just pray and meditate everyday?'

Whenever I spoke to her, it was like: 'So, Mum, what are you up to this week?' And she'd say: 'Well, I'm going to a funeral on Thursday and then I have another one coming up on Monday.' She loved it. She loved helping families organise funerals and helping them through their grief. I think that part of it was that she lost her own mother when she was twelve. She died of an asthma attack when she was forty-four, leaving five kids behind.

It's a massive thing to lose your mother, obviously. It affected everyone in the family and continues to have a lasting impact. It probably made her an anxious person. Of course, everyone is diagnosed with anxiety these days and we live in an anxious age. Apparently, we are making more decisions in a year than our grandparents made in a lifetime – or some shit like that. Everyone deals with things in their own way.

There are a few significant Olives in Australian history. Olive Pink was an anthropologist, and Olive Cotton was an amazing photographer – the female Max Dupain, but obviously has only gained the deserved recognition in more recent times. Then there's Olive Oyl, Popeye's girlfriend, and the myopic, buck-toothed Olive in *On The Buses*. I'm not sure she was a feminist.

Mum was always impatient for change and success. I think I would say that's the main difference between men and women – and there is obviously a huge grey area at either pole – but men tend to be happy with the status quo and avoid changing, and women want to change everything. Let's change the kitchen, the bathroom, let's make this relationship better, let's move, let's change something. Mum always wanted change.

Mum and Dad had some friends who had come from a similar area in the UK and they were all intensely private people. They are, in fact, secretive, to a point. My parents were always saying things like:

'Don't tell people what you're up to.'

'Don't reveal too much.'

'Never discuss money.'

'Never discuss your politics.'

'Never say where you're going.'

I don't know where all that came from. I think that advice actually bears up to an extent, because there is not much to be gained by spilling your guts and telling your life story to every idiot. It's a good idea to maintain that sense of self.

In comedy, I do none of that. I tell everyone everything – but I am an idiot.

Mum shakes her head. She can't believe it. 'What are you saying about us?' She feels quite exposed by it. There's a degree of pride, though, too. People at the parish will say: 'I saw him on television,' and she just raises her eyebrows and says: 'What was he saying?' I guess she enjoys the notoriety to an extent.

Dad died a long time ago – in 1987. I was twenty-two and mum was only fifty-five. He died of a heart attack out of the blue. He didn't look unfit, but probably with the worry and stress of migrating and making sure his three boys got through – I think there is a lot of pressure on the male psyche in that regard.

I didn't really know how to grieve – I was so busy with repressing most of my emotions. We were very protective of Mum. She went back to work but she was broken.

When I was little I had a hole in my ear drum and terrible abscesses – it was horrible pain – and Mum would spend hours with me at night singing hymns, which is a good way of soothing the soul, so I've got a lot of Catholic liturgy up my sleeve. There are lots of hymns that are imprinted on my middle ear.

Mum's Catholicism is an intrinsic part of her, so I can't say where the religion ends and the person begins. It's just a part of her life. She wanted all of us to go to church every week and she was quietly keen for me to become a priest. I was into the magical thinking of it for a while, but it wasn't a path I was ever going to take.

Her brand of religion is very much about her soul and, you know, prayer. And prayer by any other name is meditation, so maybe it was the most calming thing in her life too. I just think that she is probably an over-thinker. It made things a challenge, sometimes. You had to remind her – not everyone is against you, not everything is going to be a catastrophe, not everything has to be achieved now, so just chill the fuck out.

Her main lesson was to do whatever it takes in this life to make yourself happy, and if something isn't working for you, cut it out. That was one of the negative things I picked up from my mother. If she didn't like someone or didn't like something, the axe would fall and that was it – done. She's a put-down-the-phone-halfway-through-the-conversation kind of person.

Close the book on it.

She doesn't reconcile.

The only person she reconciles with is God. She does not reconcile with anyone. If you have an argument with my mother, you've got to be prepared to do the making up or you're done. Hard and fast.

In certain friendships and certain relationships with people, I have fallen into the trap of doing that, too. But I recognise that it's not an adult way to conduct yourself, so I'm very conscious of it.

I think in every child-parent relationship, the child raises the parent to an extent and then sees what they don't want – 'I'm not doing that, that's appalling.' That's when you start to find your own way.

Mum has sisters. There was one in Melbourne, one in

Adelaide and then two siblings stayed in the UK. She never saw her sisters much – they were a feuding bunch. My brothers and I were conscious of that. We maintain contact, we maintain closeness and if there is a ripple or some kind of irritation we sort it out. Or, we just let a little bit of time sit and then make contact. My mum's mum died when she was twelve and that changes everything forever; my brothers and I didn't have to cope with such tectonic shifts and massive turbulence. You know, those rumbles in families where all the relationships start changing? In Mum's family, those relationships all had fault lines – and big fault lines, too. And Mum is stubborn, so things don't get sorted out.

'No, I'm not calling her, why should I, she can call me.' She'd say childish stuff that's maybe frozen in amber from when her mum died. Losing your mum – what an awful thing to happen to a person.

I'd say: 'Mum, it's your sister – you know, there is not a huge amount of time left. Call her – maybe call her every day, it doesn't matter who caused it.'

But she was always like: '*She* can call *me* if she's that desperate.' Oh man, she's so steadfast. She's almost soviet in her refusal to accept responsibility.

There was never any pressure to get married or have children. That question – 'Have you got a girlfriend?' – was never asked of any of us. I can never remember that being asked.

Mum is crazy proud of us all and she is especially complimentary about the way I have raised my daughters. She talks about those girls with so much pride – they're so kind, they communicate so beautifully, they've got great manners, they are so generous and sensitive about other people's feelings. And most of those things that I've articulated – my mum would never see herself that way, and she's all of those things.

Her grandmother role has been limited. She did a very interesting thing when we were leaving her to move out of home and that was reclaiming her life. She said: 'You have no obligation to me – you don't have to come around here and see me all the time, or call me all the time, just go on with your life. I'm your mum, but I don't want to speak to you every day and I certainly don't want you visiting me and bothering me all the time.' Which was her way of saying: 'You're free.'

She had obviously seen that mother's claim on children and the guilt that it can cause, and was determined not to let it happen to us. She didn't want a part of it, and she didn't want to be some doting, babysitting grandmother, so she was more like: 'I want to see my grandkids, but, you know, all in good time – they've got their own lives to lead as well.'

I speak to her weekly, and I see her biweekly or monthly. And Mum's fine with that. She has never come to see stand-up at a pub or club. She doesn't do pubs or comedy clubs – she thinks they're common.

And that is a word that my Mum would use. 'Don't be common.'

Jesus – common?

She's always come to the Comedy Festival shows because the festival is a different thing. It's more of a theatrical landscape and fits in with her feeling of what *isn't* common. I know she's seen me on TV but she doesn't stop everything to watch every time. She's definitely no scrapbook-keeper.

She has led a very independent life. I admire that.

Her attitude is: 'I've made my decisions, you make your decisions and we're all fine with that.' To an extent, that sounds kind of cold, but I think that it's actually a brave and realistic thing to do because the alternative is that we can emotionally manipulate each other until the end.

The result is that I don't feel like there's that reciprocity required. She has truly set me free – we can actually love unconditionally. It's an incredibly fabulous way to be.

She's also taught me that confronting a situation is probably the best way to go, rather than putting up with it. By her own philosophy, she's taught me not to put up with her bullshit, though her ways are brutal. She's got the stomach for it – I think I'm a little more conciliatory.

If it's not working for you, change it – or get out. I've done that in my own relationships. I'll bear up for a while but if it's not getting better then, you know.

Mum was always of the opinion that relationships are meant to make life better. They're not meant to be painful torturous things that put people in conflict. I know I'm not the easiest person to have a relationship with and I think that that's very good advice.

There was no lack of discipline in our household. It was the good old-fashioned 1960s and 1970s, where you would occasionally get whacked. If there was an injustice against one of her children, though, it was heartening to watch her fly at teachers or whoever was responsible – in her way. There were no expletives, no raised voice – she'd just coldly look into their eyes and say: 'That's not going to happen again, you understand what I'm saying?' and we'd be standing beside her, like: 'Our mum is the shit, yeah.'

My brother and I used to walk ourselves home from school together and then let ourselves in. Wednesdays was spaghetti bol night and so she taught us how to make spaghetti bolognese. She also taught us how to do the washing up, put on a load of washing, hang it out, iron straight, vacuum. That was another thing – we are all domestically equipped. We are three boys who live in very tidy houses. There's never clothes or towels on the floor – 'Towels don't go on the floor!' We are all probably a little uptight domestically. Because we were taught: that's the way to do it.

I think, to an extent, the modern man has been a massive beneficiary of feminism because we've learned to spend more time with our children, look after our health, talk about our sex lives, examine our inner feelings and our attitudes towards women. Yes, Mum would identify as a feminist – absolutely. And she was a massive fan of Germaine Greer.

Another great lesson my mother gave me? Because I'm in a second relationship and I was discussing having a child with my wife, Mum told me: 'There's always room for a baby,' and that's a very nice Catholic opinion to have.

I was scared and anxious about the whole thing playing out again like the first time around, and so she made me answer this question: 'What kind of man would deny a woman the right to have a baby?'

I went: 'Is the answer a weak man?'

'Yes,' she said. 'That is the correct answer – so what do you want to be?'

'Not a weak man.'

'Yes.'

And she's right. If you don't want a child and your partner does, then get out of the relationship. Don't convince somebody not to have a child.

So that's it – that's Olive in a nutshell.

A terrible thing I remember is Mum threatening us with: 'One day I'll put my coat on…' Mind you, she was raising three boys and it was a bit of a shit fight at times – she'd say: 'I'll put my coat on, walk through that door and I won't be coming back.'

That deeply affected me and I'd look at my brothers and they would be like: 'Don't worry, she won't be going anywhere.'

CLAIRE HALLIDAY

What did Claire Halliday's mother teach her? That people are complex and have reasons behind the things they say and do. Claire's career as a feature writer for some of Australia's leading magazines and newspapers has been built on the idea that everyone has a story. In the case of her own mother, it's definitely true.

M um's in her late eighties now and I'm still learning about life from her. Some of the most confronting lessons have been intensely personal ones. I have learned to admit to faults in my own behaviour and the way I've reacted in different situations, and acknowledge that there have been times I could have chosen to be more polite, or more patient. Not just with my parents, but everyone.

But I've also learned that regret is a wasted feeling. You can't change the past. What you can change is the way you respond to the events in your life and how you choose to live the rest of it. For a long time – right up until I was in my mid-forties –

Pictured: Vilma Halliday

when I was around Mum for any length of time, I'd adopt the attitude and tone of a snappy, sullen teenager. It was like our relationship was trapped in 1985 and we were both still carrying old tensions into every new interaction.

Up until about three years ago, when we finally found some fantastic accommodation that we can return to when we visit from Melbourne every year, my husband and I used to cram into Mum's house each summer to stay in Adelaide for Christmas – two kids and two adults squished into my old bedroom and the two little ones sleeping with Mum in her bed.

It wouldn't take long for the niggling to start – I would get too easily frustrated and she would react to me also. They're not my husband's best holiday memories.

But there are lots of good times to look back on. Childhood for me was fantastic. Classic 1970s memories of beach holidays and freedom to roam around with the neighbourhood kids and come home to a mum who was always home. Mum did work part-time by the time we'd been at primary school for a couple of years but she was always there to see us off to school and always there to welcome us back home again. It felt safe.

I gave Mum a hard time when I was a teenager. Now that I have four children of my own – including two teenagers – I can't imagine how I would cope if they did one quarter of the things I got up to. I'm lucky they're using their energies in different ways – for now, at least. I was all about being as outrageous and challenging as possible, and I was angry. She was too, in many ways. It takes all the knowledge I have as an adult, with all the things I have learned about myself, her life, and the world in general, to really understand that.

It was the perfect storm, really. Mum was 40 when I came

along and so by the time I hit the teen years and got my period, she was going through menopause – a house with two females navigating their own versions of hormonal stress, with the added tension of me not handling various events in my life and acting out pretty badly. It wouldn't have been fun for her.

I was eleven when I found out I was adopted. I'd forgotten the age detail but a few years ago I reconnected with one of my best primary school friends, thanks to social media, and he told me he could remember the day I came back to school – he said it was grade six – and told him all about it.

I had always felt different in some way within my family – through no fault of my mum, dad or my older brother – and so when I decided to turn the little key in Mum's locked bedroom drawers one day when she was at work, and I found the adoption certificate amongst the other papers there, those feelings I'd had made more sense. At the same time, it was still a shock, and I spent the next few years feeling displaced and pretty confused about a lot of things. I switched between romanticising the ideas about why my birth mother might have had to put me up for adoption – almost against her will because of pressure from strict parents, perhaps – to feeling completely let down that she hadn't loved me enough to want to keep me for herself. I took those feelings out on Mum – my adoptive mother. It was a weird time.

I went from being pretty much a straight-A student in primary school to being on the brink of adolescence with this news that I wasn't completely who I thought I was.

By the time I was in my second year of high school, I'd begun reinventing myself any way I could. I'd cut and dyed my hair, pierced my ears too many times, failed lots of the subjects I'd stopped caring about, became a vegetarian, wagged school, and had taken to my room with a record player to obsess over meaningful lyrics and dream of being a rock journalist.

I think most teenagers feel a distance from their parents at some point. I just didn't get Mum at all. The best anecdote to show how different I felt from her is all about the Beatles. I'd discovered their music in a major way. Most bands I loved tracked their influences, in some form, to some aspects of the Beatles. They were – and still are – my favourite band. A cool bit of Adelaide-related Beatles trivia is that, when the band came to Australia in 1964, Adelaide actually gave them the biggest crowd they ever had anywhere in the world. They stood on the balcony of the Adelaide Town Hall and 300,000 people packed the streets to see them. Before that moment, there was a motorcade from the airport in open-top convertibles and people lined the main road to the city, the Anzac Highway, to watch them drive past. The Anzac Highway is about a two-minute walk from my childhood home, where Mum still lives, and so I asked Mum to tell me about the time she saw The Beatles go past. But she didn't see them go past. Mum had a hairdressing appointment. She was at the hairdresser – on the Anzac Highway – and wasn't fussed about any of it. It meant nothing to her. I still get frustrated thinking about it.

By the time I was in high school, my Dad was running the sheet metal engineering business that he'd inherited from his father into the ground through some silly business decisions. Dad had an increasingly slack attitude to his understanding of his own value and the quality of work he provided for people – poor Mum had to deal with the worry of unpaid invoices from customers and a growing amount of debt. To say Dad was an alcoholic paints a picture of a raging, angry drunk, and life wasn't like that at all, but he did drink too much and it did have an impact. He would head to the factory at 6 a.m., do a few hours work, then disappear. Mum was working at the factory as his receptionist and office admin person and she would be left there, dealing with the guys on the floor, who gradually became fewer and fewer as the work dried up. She found out later that Dad would be at the pub down the road when it opened at 11 a.m. – having a quiet wine or two and chatting the other barflies. He'd head back to the factory, do a bit more work, head home by 3 p.m. or so, start on the cask wine, and shortly after dinner he'd be ready for bed. Mum would be left on the couch to watch TV by herself.

She must have felt really lonely, but I was too wrapped up in my teenage problems to realise it, and I'm sure my attitude just added to it. From my perspective, I was caught up in feelings of: 'I don't belong here.' I wasted lots of time wondering how I had ended up in this very suburban, working-class family. I felt like I was meant to be part of a bigger life, somehow. I felt trapped.

Once I turned eighteen, I was able to apply for non-identifying information to find out some of the basic details about the people who had conceived me. I received the reply – a letter that told me the height and hair colour and age of both my birth mother and birth father, and I remember feeling like it was something I couldn't discuss with Mum. She just shut down anytime I tried to talk about anything to do with adoption and wanting to find out more about where I came from. I felt like I was betraying her.

I'm not sure what I was hoping to find, or what I thought

would happen to my life. I think I was longing to find out that my 'real' mother was an artist and my dad was a writer or something – anything that would make me feel like all the creative dreams I had about writing and music and film-making might have had an origin somewhere – but the news was that she was a 19-year-old nurse and he was a 21-year-old postal worker. And they were both short – and from Tasmania. I remember feeling disappointed I had come from such mundane stock.

When the adoption laws changed in South Australia a few years later, I took the next step and applied for my birth certificate to find out my birth mother's name, but I didn't tell Mum at first.

I'd seen lots of adoption reunion stories on midday movies so I was under the impression that I'd have this amazing reconnection with my birth mother. The reality was that she wasn't interested at all. Once I had her full name, which was a bit unusual, it only took me about half an hour of detective work at the local post office – before the days of the internet – looking at interstate phone books and making a few phone calls before I found her address and number. I went home and called her straight away. In hindsight, I should have thought more about what to say but I just couldn't. I felt like I'd already been waiting my whole life. That phone call was the most difficult, most awkward call I've ever made. It's a blur now but she must have asked for my address because a couple of days later a letter arrived in the mail. Just two small, firmly worded pages of neat cursive handwriting, but packed with a lot of information. She told me that I shouldn't cry for what I didn't have. Her own mother had died when she was a little girl and she told me that I should be grateful to have been chosen by a nice family and have a mother who'd adopted me.

The distance between Mum and I was huge by that time and I'd already moved out of home to live with some friends in a share-house, so it was something I kept mostly to myself. By then I had immersed myself in the world of seeing live bands and being obsessed with the boys who played in them, playing the part of the unhappy young woman with low self-esteem, looking for someone to love me. There was always this feeling that Mum couldn't possibly understand any of my feelings or what it was like to be me. Most children have that idea about their parents, I suppose. You tend to be quite self-centred when you're young.

I think, generally, kids have a way of taking their parents for granted and not showing any interest in their lives or background or experiences. I see that myself with my own children. They don't mean to be disinterested in a rude way – they just have other things on their minds and they don't seem that keen to find out about the life you might have lived before you became their mum.

Who knows what I'll tell them about all the details of my life if they eventually ask? There are definitely some things I'd rather they never knew.

I remember conversations with Mum about her childhood here and there – I was always fascinated by hearing tales of her growing up in WWII and what it was like to have two older brothers away at war, plus a dad who was sent to Darwin to do his duties as an older man on the home front. Mum and her mother were home alone in Adelaide for most of the war.

Mum loved her parents and her brothers so much. As her mum and dad aged they came to live next door in the maisonette that was attached to our own maisonette and when my Pa eventually died in his sleep there one night, Mum took on the role of carer for her own mother. When my grandmother's dementia got too bad, she had to go into a nursing home, and I remember a real sadness about Mum when both of her parents were dead.

Losing both her brothers over the years was something that also had a huge impact on her. It must be strange to be the last one alive in your family. There are so many stories and memories that just stop being revisited when the people who lived them with you aren't there anymore. Then, when my dad died about twelve years ago, Mum had to create new routines.

Mum had always told me that her family was fairly poor growing up. I knew she had always studied dancing and wanted to be a ballerina but didn't really have the money for proper tuition and training – something I think was one of the biggest sadnesses of her life. Mum also loved classical music – we had music playing at home every evening when I was a kid. Dad's tastes would be for artists like Frank Sinatra and Cleo Laine and Glenn Campbell and John Denver – and Mum loved them too – but when it was just her she'd put on records of Vivaldi's Four Seasons, or pieces by Mozart and Tchaikovsky. She's told me lots of times – even recently – about how they once had a piano in their house that they were looking after for one of her aunts, and how she'd always wanted to play it and that the lady down the street had offered to give her lessons. Mum was really excited about it but then her aunt decided to take the piano back. 'And that was the end of me playing the piano,' Mum says.

Mum also talked a lot about her days as an usherette at the

old Regent Cinema in Adelaide and, weirdly, I had a part-time job there as an usherette myself when I was about eighteen. She loved her days at the Regent. I think she worked there through her mid-twenties into her early thirties before she married my dad. For years, she's always attended at least a couple of reunion lunches each year. I think they've only petered out in the last few years. Almost all of her friends have died now. She's one of the only ones left.

She's never driven a car so she gets around on public transport and has always been very active. One day she's on a tram to the city, or to the beach for a walk along the jetty, another day she gets picked up by the council bus to go to a community lunch; she has line dancing class another day and she also goes swimming with some other people around her age in an aqua exercise class. Then she volunteers at the local primary school one morning a week – reading with the grade one and grade two classes. That's starting to slow down now, though. She's not really enjoying life in the same way she used to. She has a favourite quote she says comes from Bette Davis: 'Old age ain't no place for sissies.'

Now that her memory is slipping away, I am kicking myself that I never sat down with her to get her stories on audio or video. You think you have time to do these things and you mean to, and then the opportunity is gone.

I moved to Melbourne when I was 21 to get away from an abusive boyfriend. I used to go back to Adelaide a couple of times a year to visit Mum and Dad and my friends, but the gap between us was a chasm at times and, even though there aren't any more fights and I call her a couple of times a week, it's never much more than surface chit-chat. She'll ask about my kids and I'll tell her and I'll ask about what she's doing that day and that's about it. We've never had that relationship where I would talk really deeply to her about anything personal and important in my life. I know friends who are like that with their mums and I kind of envy it but I admit that, in part, it was my own making.

When I was in my mid-twenties, a big secret came out that gave us all a shock.

I'd just been for a visit and then the phone rang a few days later and Mum told me she'd pay for me to come back on the plane because she had something really important she needed to tell me face-to-face. I remember thinking that one of my parents must be dying – cancer or something – but she wouldn't share anything on the phone so I booked my flight and headed back to see what the fuss was.

I'd barely set foot in their kitchen when she blurted it out. She'd had a baby with another man she'd had an affair with – before marrying my dad – and she'd become pregnant and given the baby up for adoption.

The reason the secret was out now was because that baby – a daughter – had tracked Mum down.

Life is full of surprises. That's something else I've learned.

The full story is that, even though Mum never had the luxury of having full-time dance training, she must have been good and she had a job as a dancer in touring musical theatre shows with JC Williamson, which was a very well-known Melbourne theatre company. She must have been incredibly naïve and got swept off her feet by one of the male dancers and they actually got married. Trouble was, he was gay, and my poor mum didn't have a clue.

So there she was, moving from Adelaide to Melbourne to dance in musicals with a theatre company that toured Australia, and married to a guy who never consummated the marriage because he didn't actually fancy women.

Mum's had a real bitterness about that, her whole life. I don't blame her. The way she found out was that she walked in on her husband in bed with another of the male dancers. And that was that. The marriage was annulled and Mum was embarrassed and devastated. He continued on with a career in theatre and ended up in London, apparently, but Mum went back to Adelaide and working at the Regent, and then ended up in an affair with the married manager.

For me, it wasn't so much the shock of finding out my mum had a baby and adopted it out that had an impact – it was that I had to watch my mum reunite and have a relationship with her own daughter. It was what I had wanted my birth mother to do with me, but mine wasn't interested at all. The daughter, Michelle, was accepted into our family with open arms by everyone and suddenly there was an extra extended family joining us for birthdays and Christmas. I think it was fantastic for Mum to reunite with her daughter. For her, it was a chapter of her life that now had some closure – there was no more wondering about what had happened to the baby she'd given up. My Dad accepted it all – everybody did. It was different for my brother too because he was Mum and Dad's natural child, whom they'd had before Mum lost another baby boy and found out she couldn't have any more children. For him, he actually found a new person he was related to, but for me, it was something more unusual and complicated.

Michelle and I got along fine but she understood my feelings of displacement. It was another dent in the relationship between Mum and I, too. I took the frustration I had for my own birth mother out on her, I guess, and all the times I felt she'd closed me off from conversations about my own adoption, I realised she must have been thinking about her own daughter out there somewhere. It's a bit of a soap opera.

Watching Mum reunite with her own birth daughter made me want to give my own birth mother reunion another chance, so I used a business trip as an excuse to contact her again. She was living in Perth, and even though my trip was to Darwin and I'd only tacked on a side flight to Perth in the hope she might see me, I rang her to say that I happened to be in town and asked her if she might have time for a coffee. I could tell she wasn't impressed, but she told me to give her twenty-four hours and she'd let me know. She did call – and gave me the name of a cafe and a time. I'd never been to Perth but when I drove the hire car into the car park of a massive shopping centre – and this was on a busy Saturday morning – and discovered the 'cafe' was little more than a coffee counter in a food court, I should have just left. But I didn't. I met my birth mother, for what I'm sure will be the only time in my life I'll ever see her. I drank a bad latte while she sipped at a cappuccino and punched out medical facts about my familial history, as if that was the only thing that must have mattered to me. I asked her to stay for a second coffee but she told me that she didn't have time because she was running late to meet her daughter and go shopping for her formal dress.

Ouch.

That was that.

I spent a lot of time taking that stuff out on Mum – I mean, my adoptive mother. My anger was misplaced. It took me ages to move on.

Now I'm in that stage of life, like a lot of my friends, where things are turning and myself and my brother are having sometimes daily conversations about Mum's health and wellbeing – wondering what can be done to get her into a nursing home, or whether that is really the right thing to do. She switches between expressing her loneliness, despite all her activities, and telling us she wants to stay living at home.

It's made me think more deeply about my own old age and how I might want to end up and things I might be able to do to try to feel happy and settled and fulfilled.

I can't predict the future but I'm hoping to live a life where I don't leave ambitions unfulfilled and to try to achieve all the things I want to do. It's what everybody wants, I suppose.

I'm not sure how my own children will judge me when I'm older – with four very different views, I presume. I figure that, as long as I am happy, I am in a better position to help them find happiness. That's all any mother wants for their children, really.